The American Novel series provides students of American literature with introductory critical guides to great works of American literature. Each volume begins with a substantial introduction by a distinguished authority on the text, giving details of the work's composition, publication history, and contemporary reception, as well as a survey of the major critical trends and readings from first publication to the present. This overview is followed by a group of new essays, each specifically commissioned from a leading scholar in the field, which together constitute a forum of interpretative methods and prominent contemporary ideas on the text. There are also helpful guides to further reading. Specifically designed for undergraduates, the series will be a powerful resource for anyone engaged in the critical analysis of major American novels and other important texts.

Ernest Hemingway is one of the most gifted, oft-taught, and frequently criticized authors of the short story in the English language. The introduction and four original scholarly essays in this volume constitute an overview of Hemingway's career as a short story writer and of practical problems involved in reading this work. The early short story "Up in Michigan" is explained in relation to the groundbreaking short story cycle *In Our Time*. Problems of narration are analyzed in "Now I Lay Me," an integral part of Hemingway's second collection of short stories, *Men without Women*. An essay on "Fathers and Sons" takes a detailed look at the ecological and Native American background of the collection *Winner Take Nothing*. "Snows of Kilimanjaro" is examined from a postcolonial perspective. Also included is a selected bibliography designed to direct readers to the most valuable resources for the study of Hemingway's short fiction.

NEW ESSAYS ON
HEMINGWAY'S SHORT FICTION

★ The American Novel ★

GENERAL EDITOR

Emory Elliott
University of California, Riverside

Other works in the series:

New Essays on
Hemingway's Short Fiction

Edited by
Paul Smith

CAMBRIDGE
UNIVERSITY PRESS

PUBLISHED BY THE PRESS SYNDICATE OF THE UNIVERSITY OF CAMBRIDGE
The Pitt Building, Trumpington Street, Cambridge, CB2 1RP, United Kingdom

CAMBRIDGE UNIVERSITY PRESS
The Edinburgh Building, Cambridge CB2 2RU, United Kingdom
40 West 20th Street, New York, NY 10011-4211, USA
10 Stamford Road, Oakleigh, Melbourne 3166, Australia

First published 1998

Printed in the United States of America

Typeset in Meridien

Library of Congress Cataloging-in-Publication Data
New essays on Hemingway's short fiction / edited by Paul Smith.
p. cm. – (The American novel)
Includes bibliographical references.
ISBN 0-521-55382-2. – ISBN 0-521-55651-1 (pbk.)
1. Hemingway, Ernest, 1899–1961 – Criticism and interpretation.
2. Short story. I. Smith, Paul, 1925 Dec. 23– II. Series.
PS3515.E37Z7467 1998
813'.52 – dc21 97-23485

*A catalog record for this book is available from
the British Library*

ISBN 0 521 55382 2 hardback
ISBN 0 521 55651 1 paperback

The great thing is to last and get your work done and see and hear and learn and understand; and write when there is something that you know; and not before; and not too damned much after. Let those who want to save the world if you can get to see it clear and as a whole. Then any part you make will represent the whole if it's made truly. The thing to do is work and learn to make it.

– Ernest Hemingway

Contents

vii

Contents

Series Editor's Preface

In literary criticism the last twenty-five years have been particularly fruitful. Since the rise of the New Criticism in the 1950s, which focused attention of critics and readers upon the text itself – apart from history, biography, and society – there has emerged a wide variety of critical methods which have brought to literary works a rich diversity of perspectives: social, historical, political, psychological, economic, ideological, and philosophical. While attention to the text itself, as taught by the New Critics, remains at the core of contemporary interpretation, the widely shared assumption that works of art generate many different kinds of interpretations has opened up possibilities for new readings and new meanings.

Before this critical revolution, many works of American literature had come to be taken for granted by earlier generations of readers as having an established set of recognized interpretations. There was a sense among many students that the canon was established and that the larger thematic and interpretative issues had been decided. The task of the new reader was to examine the ways in which elements such as structure, style, and imagery contributed to each novel's acknowledged purpose. But recent criticism has brought these old assumptions into question and has thereby generated a wide variety of original, and often quite surprising, interpretations of the classics, as well as of rediscovered works such as Kate Chopin's *The Awakening*, which has only recently entered the canon of works that scholars and critics study and that teachers assign their students.

The aim of The American Novel Series is to provide students of American literature and culture with introductory critical guides to American novels and other important texts now widely read and studied. Usually devoted to a single work, each volume begins with an introduction by the volume editor, a distinguished authority on the text. The introduction presents details of the work's composition, publication history, and contemporary reception, as well as a survey of the major critical trends and readings from first publication to the present. This overview is followed by four or five original essays, specifically commissioned from senior scholars of established reputation and from outstanding younger critics. Each essay presents a distinct point of view, and together they constitute a forum of interpretative methods and of the best contemporary ideas on each text.

It is our hope that these volumes will convey the vitality of current critical work in American literature, generate new insights and excitement for students of American literature, and inspire new respect for and new perspectives upon these major literary texts.

Emory Elliott
University of California, Riverside

1

Introduction: Hemingway and the Practical Reader

PAUL SMITH

TWENTY years ago common knowledge told us that there was nothing more to be said about Hemingway's fiction: The patterns were clear; motifs, categorized. We had an authorized biography and what seemed to be stable texts. Then, just as our beliefs were beginning to harden into dogma, Hemingway's manuscripts and unpublished letters were opened to scholars and revisionist work opened the fiction to new readings. A cottage industry was born. Those academics, myself included, who moved into that virtual village found overwhelming evidence that every Hemingway text was flawed in its publishing, that the author was more literate and complex than we suspected, and that there was much in his fiction we had ignored. My contribution to this endeavor has focused almost entirely on reading Hemingway's rather amazing short fiction, which I have argued was his real genius, transforming as it did the way American writers tell stories. In the opening lines of *The Making of Americans*, Gertrude Stein writes of an angry son dragging his father through his own orchard. " 'Stop!' cried the groaning old man at last, 'Stop! I did not drag my father beyond this tree.' " This parable might well be the epigraph for this book. When asked to edit a collection of new essays on Hemingway's short fiction, I solicited submissions from five diverse, rigorous, and talented scholars, challenging them and myself to take you, my practical reader, beyond your previous limits.

Let me explain myself. The *Hemingway* of my title refers to both the writer and his fiction. I make this point because I want to consider at times what he wrote in letters, articles, and memoirs about his fiction, and at others, the fiction itself. For "the reader" I have you in mind (like Whitman, I feel your eyes upon my page), a "practical" reader who will agree that reading fiction once took, and with any luck still takes, practice. Not, however, so practical as to oppose all speculation or theory, for reading itself is speculative, and it's been said that there is nothing so practical as a good theory.

In raising some questions about reading Hemingway, I take as my text a passage from *Studies in Classic American Literature* where D. H. Lawrence warns a practical reader of his generation:

> An artist is usually a damned liar, but his art, if it be art, will tell you the truth of his day. . . . Never trust the artist. Trust the tale. The proper function of a critic is to save the tale from the artist who created it. (12, 13)

Lawrence's striking prose seems at first to dare us to step outside and settle the matter, and this reader is practical enough to agree; after all, Lawrence is an artist himself, and if it takes one to know one, then, yes, they are liars and not to be trusted. We can all cite an occasion when a writer assured an audience that some profound work is really very simple: Robert Frost often claimed that "Stopping by Woods" was just a poem about a fellow who wanted to get the hell home. Then, again, if all artists are liars, and Lawrence is an artist, is his remark that artists are liars itself a lie? No, for it's as if Lawrence acquitted himself as one of those artists who are only "usually" liars – you know, only now and then.

By now, any practical reader has become a bit skittish. There is a way out of this quandary, as is often so when we're faced with only two options. Why not use the tale to discover whether to trust the artist? If the art will tell us the truth of the artist's "day" – whatever that may be – it should tell us if the artist is to be trusted. Begin with the fiction, the story, and if what it tells us is confirmed by anything the writer might have said of it, so much the better; if not, then take Lawrence at his word. A sensible attitude, I think, and not out of order in reading Hemingway.

2

The Theory of Omission and "Out of Season"

Working on the memoir *A Moveable Feast* in the summer of 1957, Hemingway discusses a moment in 1924 when he remembered writing a story in the late spring of 1923:

> It was a very simple story called "Out of Season" and I had omitted the real end of it which was that the old man hanged himself. This was omitted on my new theory that you could omit anything if you knew that you omitted and the omitted part would strengthen the story and make people feel something more than they understood. (75)

A "simple" story, yes, of course, but how that word "theory" seems to leap at us out of what is some rather lame prose. If what we are being told is that an implication we discover as readers is often more persuasive than a writer's statement, it might have been new to Hemingway but to few others and it would hardly count as a theory.

Consider the story. "Out of Season" is one of the three in Hemingway's *Three Stories & Ten Poems* (published in 1923), and like the other two it stakes out scenes he would explore in later stories: in "Up in Michigan," the small villages and surrounding woods in northern Michigan where he spent his boyhood summers; in "My Old Man," the realm of sport and gambling – here, horse racing; and in "Out of Season," the stations, hotels, and favored haunts of the American tourist in Europe. "Out of Season" opens on a cold and overcast spring day in Cortina d'Ampezzo in the Italian Dolomites. Peduzzi, a local character, has spent the morning spading a hotel garden for four lire, getting drunk on his pay, and arranging to guide a young gentleman and his wife to a trout stream after lunch. He has three more grappas, and they join him to walk through the town to the Hotel Concordia. As they enter the hotel bar to buy some marsala wine, there is tension between the couple. The husband is barely apologetic; the wife's still embittered over something he said at lunch. They walk with Peduzzi to the stream. The couple argue over fishing with a drunk for a guide before the season legally opens, and the wife leaves. The young man prepares to fish but neither he nor his guide has remembered to bring the lead sinkers, so he and Peduzzi finish the marsala. Peduzzi plans the fishing for the next day; the young man gives him four lire, and the story ends as Peduzzi promises that

> "I will have minnows, Signor. Salami, everything. You and I and the Signora. The three of us."
> "I may not be going," said the young gentleman, "very probably not. I will leave word with the padrone at the hotel office." (*Complete Stories* 139)

I cite the story's conclusion because it is from there that the narrative directs us to imagine what might happen in the silent future, speculation crucial for the concept underlying the theory of omission.

Nearly a decade after writing that story in the late spring of 1923, Hemingway first mentioned the theory in *Death in the Afternoon* (1932), and then only in passing and with no mention of "Out of Season." In 1958, three years before his death, he referred to the theory as it applied to *The Old Man and the Sea* (*Paris Review* 125). Then, in the posthumous *A Moveable Feast* (1964), the theory was associated with this story to become in time something of an axiom in Hemingway criticism. And there's fair warning, for what yesterday's criticism takes as self-evident is often what tomorrow's will challenge. The counter-evidence came to light later in Hemingway's own letters and manuscripts. In a letter to F. Scott Fitzgerald (ca. 24 December 1925) Hemingway described the occasion that inspired "Out of Season." The story was, he said, an almost literal transcription of what happened.

> Your ear is always more acute when you are upset by a row of any sort, . . . and when I came in from the unproductive fishing trip I wrote that story right off on the typewriter without punctuation. . . . I [had] reported [the guide] to the hotel owner . . . and he fired him and as . . . he was quite drunk and very desperate, [he] hanged himself in a stable. . . . I wanted to write a tragic story without violence. So I didn't put in the hanging. Maybe that sounds silly. I didn't think the story needed it. (*Selected Letters*, 180–1)

On the face of it, this letter seems to confirm Hemingway's later memory. Hemingway did have a good ear for dialogue whatever

4

his mood; the story's only manuscript shows that it was written rapidly without punctuation and immediately revised on the typewriter; and that he was angry after that row, for he struck the typewriter keys so hard that some of the letters punched holes in the paper (Kennedy Library/EH 644).

But imagine what had to have happened if Hemingway did angrily type the story right after the day's fishing and then deliberately omitted the hanging, for whatever effect. After reporting the "real" Peduzzi's behavior to the padrone, he began typing furiously, and then: The padrone sought out the guide and fired him on the spot; the guide became terribly depressed, raced to the stable and hanged himself. He was found almost immediately by someone who reported the news to the padrone; the padrone then, quite naturally, informed the guest who had made the original complaint; and, after all this, Hemingway turned back to his story, thought about the hanging in the light of his new theory and decided to omit it. Maybe this scenario sounds silly. If so, we should recall that Hemingway was in his early twenties when he wrote the letter, and that Fitzgerald, however much a friend, was also a writer, a competitor only three years older who had published two volumes of stories and three novels, the latest *The Great Gatsby* (1925). The letter was written in response to Fitzgerald's rating of the *In Our Time* stories just recently published. Maybe Hemingway was trying to impress Fitzgerald; maybe he was merely joking, making fun of slick magazine fiction. Maybe he was thinking more about "Big Two-Hearted River," which he himself rated as the best in the collection.

Whatever Hemingway's motive, the practical reader is fairly driven to agree with Lawrence and to trust the tale, for *if something has been left out that implies more than we know, some vestige of it, some trace, must have been left behind in the story to initiate the implication.* Few readers can find anything in "Out of Season" to imply that Peduzzi would be fired, or that he might hang himself, certainly not on that day, for he has earned as much for simply walking to the river as he did in a morning spading the garden. What, then, does the story imply? However much Peduzzi's vinous garrulity intrudes on the scene, the story is not about him but about the benighted couple. Nearly everything in the setting and the action of the story, from its title to its final lines, points to the hopelessness of their marriage. They have come to the perfect place to foreshadow their separation, for here three dialects merge but none of the three characters either listens to or understands what the others say. They arrive at the perfect time of year for such miscommunication, for like the fishing, they, too, are "out of season." Perhaps the story's final irony is that only Peduzzi, deep in his cups, has any hope for the morrow: "The three of us," he exclaims. But with the singular pronoun, "I may not be going," the young gentleman belies that hope and directs our attention toward his own lonely prospect.

Dimensions in the Stories and "The Killers"

There is a second passage in *A Moveable Feast* that, like the remark on the theory of omission, has started a good many critical hares. Hemingway is describing how in his early days he sometimes had difficulty beginning his stories if he wrote "elaborately, or like someone introducing or presenting something," but usually could overcome the difficulty if he discarded those elaborations to "start with the first true simple declarative sentence" he had written and go on from there. That led him to recall that when he finished writing a story he put it out of his mind and walked through the streets of Paris, often to the Musée du Luxembourg to see the Impressionist paintings. He was especially drawn to the Cézannes, because, as he remembered it,

I was learning something from the painting of Cézanne that made writing simple true sentences far from enough to make the stories have the *dimensions* that I was trying to put in them. . . . I was not articulate enough to explain it to anyone. Besides it was a secret. (my italics, 12, 13)

What was he learning from Cézanne and why was it a secret? The original 1924 ending of "Big Two-Hearted River," which was replaced before the story was published, tells us more. In that discarded fragment which appeared posthumously, Nick says,

It was easy to write if you used the tricks . . . Joyce had invented hundreds of them. . . . They would all turn into clichés. . . . Cézanne started with all the tricks. Then he broke the whole thing down and built the real thing. . . . He, Nick, wanted to write about country so it would be there like Cézanne had done it in painting. . . . There wasn't any trick. Nobody had ever written about country like that. He felt almost holy about it. It was a thing you couldn't talk about. (*Nick Adams Stories* 239)

This manuscript ending both explains and dramatizes the harsh imperative for originality that literary Paris in the 1920s demanded, and why, if one writer thought he had discovered a way to achieve it from Cézanne, he would hold it as a secret. What the manuscript does not explain, and there has been a good deal of critical commentary to make up for that omission, is what precisely Hemingway learned from Cézanne, and why he turned to a painter as his master in the first place.

Hemingway's young writer, too often identified with the author himself, has an almost religious zeal to be the Cézanne of modern prose, writing about landscape so that it becomes the "real thing," and just before the manuscript ends, it happens: Nick saw "how Cézanne would do the stretch of river and the swamp, stood up, and stepped down into the stream. The water was cold and actual. He waded across the stream, moving in the picture" (240). At that dramatic moment, when the cold and actual stream in the virtual prose becomes a holograph painting into which the fisherman steps, Hemingway's young artist has come close to realizing his ambition.

The reader, perhaps practical to a fault, might suspect that if one's ambition is to be more original than Joyce after *Ulysses,* there would be few masters if any to follow, discounting the fact that any writer one took as a master would be a writer still. So, choose a great artist, dead but not too dead, and if it is "dimensions" you feel your stories need, who else but one known for the geometric forms underlying his landscapes; Cézanne. That is one way to argue from the author's comment on the story, or at least from whatever he had in mind for the word "dimension."

Another way, perhaps more practical, would reverse the critical direction by beginning with what the word might refer to in a story and work back to the meaning it might have in a Cézanne painting. At the outset it is obvious that the word *dimension* is more commonly applied to a painting, and for the very good reason that art is spatial, the painting is perceived in space, however much our eyes may be directed first to a certain shape or color, then to the next, and at last to another. In reading a work of fiction, however, we begin by perceiving the story unfolding in linear time: first that happened, then that, now this. Our minds are mostly concerned with what will happen next. After we've read something, we may recall that experience as it occurred, but now, with nothing left to happen next, we are more concerned with what it means, as if it resides in some timeless space. Often, to express that meaning, we draw a diagram – a triangle to represent a conflict, circles to suggest the differing social worlds, a broken line for an action, metaphors in space for what happened in time, serving to describe the relationship among the parts of the story's "structure."

The structure in a Hemingway story can usually be described, conventionally enough, with a set of scenes marked by a change in setting or by a change of characters. What is unconventional, and so inscribes his fiction as modernist, is that the scenes often are juxtaposed with little transition and less logic to effect or explain their sequence or rationale. Such a structure may result from his prose style with its syntax linking sentences and clauses by simple, at times temporal, but rarely logical or subordinating, conjunctions. This is not to say that the structures of the stories lack form or significant pattern. Recall the pattern of the scenes in "Out of Season": five conventional scenes, the central one of which (the couple's conversation in the Concordia) is embedded between two scenes in which they walk with Peduzzi to the river. These two scenes are in turn embedded between two scenes in which the young gentleman and his guide open and close the story. This simple pattern turns the reader's attention to that crucial and literally central moment in the hotel bar when the wife utters that terrible condemnation of their relationship, "None of it makes any difference" (*Complete Stories* 137). If that is the sort of dimension, more than a sequence of true sentences, that Hemingway felt his stories needed, he might well have learned the technique from Cézanne or, indeed, from any other artist, for that dimensionality in both painting and prose directs our attention to the telling point in the narrative or on the canvas.

One of Hemingway's most familiar stories, "The Killers," offers a perfect example of a narrative that challenges and rewards the reader's perception of its structure, partly because, although its suspense is literally almost killing, not very much happens. (In most Hemingway short stories very little *happens*.) The first scene opens with two strangers entering Henry's lunchroom, where George is waiting on Nick Adams at the counter. The strangers, Al and Max, try unsuccessfully to order from the dinner menu, then settle for sandwiches, after which their small talk turns ugly. Al takes Sam the cook and Nick into the kitchen, gags and ties them up, and then he and Max reveal that they are waiting to kill Ole Andreson when he comes in at six. As evening approaches and others arrive for dinner, George tells them the cook is away or makes them a sandwich. When Ole Andreson does not arrive, the killers leave. The second scene is some twenty-five lines of dialogue: Sam says he doesn't want any more of that; George tells Nick he ought to go see Ole; Sam says he ought to stay out of it, but Nick leaves to tell Ole. In the third scene, at Hirsch's rooming house, Nick talks briefly with the landlady, Mrs. Bell, and then to Ole in his room. He tells him about the two men waiting to kill him, and offers to tell the police; but Ole, lying on his bed and looking at the wall, says that he got in wrong, there's nothing to do, and he's through running. Nick leaves after a brief conversation with Mrs. Bell. The fourth and final scene is another twenty-five lines of dialogue back at Henry's. Sam won't listen to it and goes to the kitchen. The story ends as Nick wonders what Ole did, and George says:

> "Double-crossed somebody. That's what they kill them for."
> "I'm going to get out of this town," Nick said.
> "Yes," said George, "That's a good thing to do."
> "I can't stand to think about him waiting in the room and knowing he's going to get it. It's too damned awful."

"Well," said George," you better not think about it."(*Complete Stories* 222)

Whatever image you have of the story's dimensions it will reflect the obvious symmetry between the two sets of two scenes in which the action of the first scene is followed by a reaction in the second. For all the impending violence and seemingly inevitable bloodshed, nothing happens: The killers don't kill and their victim still lies with his face to the wall. Even in the two scenes of reaction, two of the three persons do nothing, only Nick acts or resolves to act. The dimensions of the story almost by default direct our attention to the story's details. And we see in the story's texture that almost every detail, from the opening moment when we see George in charge of Henry's lunchroom to the moment when Nick assumes that Mrs. Bell is in charge of Mrs. Hirsch's rooming house, seems to have some counterpart serving as its agent: Al and Max are indistinguishable, dressed like "twins" or a "vaudeville team," even their sandwich orders are interchanged; there isn't much difference between the reactions of Sam, the cook, who denies that anything has happened, and George's dismissive explanations of the killers' motives. On the face of the wall clock, which is fast, every minute stands for twenty minutes earlier.

Reminiscent of the settings in a Franz Kafka story or a Harold Pinter play, the world of this story is not so much reflected as it is refracted, as if in a cracked mirror. Within this world two characters are intimately joined, Ole Andreson, the victim, and Nick Adams, his lonely representative, who will bear the image of the doomed boxer into his maturity. There's a good deal more one could say, as there always is with a fine work of fiction, but this much may suggest the ways in which the simple structures of Hemingway's stories, the geometric design of their scenes, direct our critical attention toward their meanings.

The Sense of Audience and "One Reader Writes"

Hemingway once promised the publisher of *In Our Time* that his stories "will be praised by highbrows and can be read by low-

10

brows," and then went on to suggest that a lowbrow was "anybody with [only] a high-school education" but left the publisher free to imagine highbrow critics writing favorable reviews (*Selected Letters* 155). More than an assurance, the remark was an accurate prediction, at least through the 1920s, of both the sales and the reviews of the two collections, *In Our Time* (1925) and *Men Without Women* (1927), and two novels, *The Sun Also Rises* (1926) and *A Farewell to Arms* (1929). But sales fell off during the hard times of the 1930s and as Hemingway turned to experiment with nonfiction in *Death in the Afternoon* (1932) and *Green Hills of Africa* (1935), his public image as the aficionado of the bullfight and the white hunter of the safari, overtook and, some would argue, overshadowed the private artist. Whether or not he invited that fame even as he fought off its invasions, his emergence as a celebrity provoked some unfavorable criticism. Two "highbrows," novelist Aldous Huxley and writer Wyndham Lewis, reviewed the cultural significance of Hemingway's characters, whom Huxley described in his essay "Foreheads Villainous Low" as unwilling or unable to admit to any intelligence or education. Lewis held that these characters were dangerously insensitive to the political drift of history and so, with no will of their own, were simply waiting to be led to slaughter; his study is called "The Dumb Ox." Both assigned these views to Hemingway himself, and so found him to be representative of a deplorable modern anti-intellectualism.

In a rather less captious way, Huxley and Lewis are right: More often than not, Hemingway's characters have little interest and less trust in the intellect, are restless in the realm of complex ideas, and discredit the rhetoric of abstractions. They are more likely to favor the emotions, the simpler intuitions, and the language of the ordinary world, a natural and common attitude for a generation whose rite of passage began in the bloodshed of the First World War. It may well be true that these attitudes reflect Hemingway's own version of anti-intellectualism that dismissed Joyce's complex literary "tricks" for the simpler dimensions in Cézanne's art. It may well explain why the "highbrow" critics and reviewers he felt would praise his stories in the 1920s became "the lice who crawl over literature" (*Green Hills* 109) in the 1930s. However, to admit that Hemingway's characters are often more passive than active, more intuitive than thoughtful, is not to suggest that what happens to them is not profound, or that their emotional reactions are any the less meaningful.

When the young gentleman in "Out of Season" tells his wife he's sorry that she feels so "rotten" and then moments later that "it's a rotten day," the simple association reveals a vista of desperation that resonates in her sense that nothing in their lives, now or ever, will make "any difference" (*Collected Stories* 137–8). When Nick Adams says that he's "going to get out of this town," his resolution has nothing to do with avoiding the killers. If he mattered at all to the implacable killers, and he does not, they would find him wherever he went, and whether he goes or not he'll always have that informing vision of the boxer with his face to the wall. In one story after another, "Indian Camp," "Soldier's Home," "Big Two-Hearted River," "Hills Like White Elephants," "A Clean, Well-Lighted Place," "The Sea Change," and beyond, little happens, and when it does, those to whom it happens do not give it much thought. Yet the stories leave us with the sense that something profoundly important, something elemental and enigmatic, has occurred and one life at least has been changed.

"One Reader Writes" offers a fair test of the sort of criticism Huxley and Lewis leveled at Hemingway. Its central character is certainly among the lowbrows, at best, and represents those to whom advice columns in the newspapers offer information and assistance. The story has been universally ignored; to this day only one critic has given it more than a passing sentence or two.[1] It opens with a paragraph describing a woman in her bedroom writing a letter with a newspaper "folded open before her and only stopping to look out of the window at the snow falling and melting on the roof as it fell."

The second paragraph is her letter, dated 6 February 1933 in Roanoke, Virginia, addressed to "Dear Doctor." It begins with a brief appeal to the doctor because she has a "decision to make and don't know just whom to trust most I dare not ask my parents, and so I come to you, and only because I need not see you can I confide in you even." Then she describes her "situation": After her sailor husband returned from three years in Shanghai, she discovered that he was taking injections for something she can't "spell . . . but it sound like this 'sifilus.'" She adds that she has not been "in close contact with him at any time since his return from China." The letter ends with an appeal to the doctor. Although her husband assures her that "it will be safe for me to live with him" she had often heard her father say that "one could well wish themselves dead if once they become a victim of that malady – I believe my Father but want to believe my Husband – Please tell me what to do – I have a daughter born while her Father was in China." The story ends as her thoughts shift from wondering whether the doctor will tell her "what's right to do" to a repeated lament that it's "such a long time though. It's a long time. My Christ it's been a long time," to the last unanswerable question:

Oh, I wish to Christ he wouldn't have got it. I don't care what he did to get it, But I wish to Christ he hadn't ever got it. It does seem like he didn't have to have got it. I don't know what to do. I wish to Christ he hadn't got any kind of malady. I don't know why he had to get a malady." (*Collected Stories* 320–21)

This working class, barely literate woman, caught between capitalized authority figures – Father and Husband – turns to higher male authority, first to an anonymous newspaper medical adviser and then to Christ Himself in her final pathetic plea, which the more literate and, yes, practical reader in those days before penicillin would recognize as hopeless. That the reader is more perceptive than the character about the nature of her husband's "malady" and the dimensions of her trapped life is as old as Chaucer's use of the "confessio" in *Canterbury Tales,* and as recent as Molly Bloom's chamber music. That the poor woman is powerless in this male world – Father, Doctor, Husband, Savior – is carefully arranged by the author to fit neatly into his 1933 collection of short stories, *Winner Take Nothing,* in which doctors, medicine, and the physical ills to which the body is vulnerable figure prominently. Never published by Hemingway as a free-standing story, "One Reader Writes" is a period piece, a product of the Great Depression, reflecting Hemingway's grow-

13

ing concern for the proletariat and his abiding interest in the female perspective. (See Liz Coates in "Up in Michigan," Jig in "Hills Like White Elephants," Harry Morgan's wife Marie in *To Have and Have Not,* Pilar in *For Whom the Bell Tolls,* and Catherine Bourne in *Garden of Eden.*)

If "One Reader Writes" still speaks to the practical reader, perhaps its structure should be given credit, for the very construction, apparently so simple, forces us to become active participants in the woman's story. All we know is this brief moment of her life: outside, snow falling to melt on the roof; inside, another of Hemingway's lonely people. First we are distanced, detached; then he moves in closer to see what she has written, then closer still, into her head, where we share her thoughts. We have only the barest sketch of how she arrived in this isolated position, but we have a pretty good idea that this story will never end happily. Hemingway has, in fact, omitted almost all of the story, leaving it to his reader to supply the beginning and the end.

The Way Stories End and "Hills Like White Elephants"

As scholars have discovered in the rich manuscript collection at the Kennedy Library, Hemingway frequently did not know or want to know a story's conclusion when he began it. In the archives there are numerous aborted stories, fragments that simply were not going anywhere that particular morning. In his early Paris period, Hemingway said:

In the morning a story starts in your head on the street car and [you] have to choke it off because it was coming so perfectly and easily and clear and right and you know that if you let it go on it will be finished and gone and you'd never be able to write it. (*Selected Letters* 104)

Sometimes this lack of foreknowledge created problems for the writer. We have all heard how he wrote over thirty endings to *A Farewell to Arms* before he was satisfied. And as we've seen above, his first ending to "Big Two-Hearted River" made that a far different story. Sometimes this mode of writing produced stories so stunning they have become our classics.

Like movies, home improvement projects, and love affairs, it is easier to start a short story than to end it effectively. Opening lines get our attention, creating in the practical reader a certain expectation. Hemingway cut away several pages of manuscript to begin "Indian Camp": "At the lake shore there was another rowboat drawn up. The two Indians stood waiting" (*Complete Stories* 67). What lake? Indians? Waiting for what, for whom? Gotcha! Once a story has gotten its hook into us, we do not expect the author to trifle with our act of attention. At the end of a life we expect the last thing said or the last act performed will be revealing. At the end of a story, which quite literally is the end of its world and the people who live there, we expect as much or more. When a story ends badly, resolving the conflict in some tawdry manner, we feel cheated. During his most productive years of reformulating the American short story, Hemingway seldom, if ever, left his reader feeling cheated. If the practical reader finishes a Hemingway story in doubt, he or she need only give careful attention to the ending, for Hemingway usually has us focused right where he wants us.

Sometimes, as in "Hills Like White Elephants," he will not tell us how the characters arrived at their present condition, or how they will resolve their conflict; we do not need to be told, for the answers are embedded in what we so briefly do see and hear. Waiting for a connecting train to Madrid, a young American couple sit at a hot way station drinking beer. On one side of the valley there "were fields of grain and trees"; on the other side, "the country was brown and dry." The couple are arguing about "an awfully simple operation." In four pages of mostly banal dialogue, the reader becomes aware that (1) the anxious woman is pregnant, (2) the insensitive man wants her to have an abortion, and (3) no matter whether she aborts the child or not, they will never be happy again. "There's nothing wrong with me," she says in the last line. "I feel fine." The practical reader, trusting the text to supply the clues, knows she is not "fine," knows that eventually she will be terribly hurt. In stories like this one,

Hemingway forces his reader to participate, to take sides, to supply answers to unvoiced questions, to understand more perhaps than his characters do. Very seldom does Hemingway ever tell you outright how you should feel about the characters or what the story means; if you bring little or no life experience to his short fiction, chances are you will read past its implications without ever knowing what you missed. If you realized, in reading "Hills Like White Elephants," that it was an abortion the couple was discussing, you supplied the missing link. In doing so, you have admitted something about yourself.

"Hills Like White Elephants" also illustrates how Hemingway learned to subvert in his early fiction the traditional endings of the short story. For stories written between 1922 and 1927, he frequently avoided the classic resolutions, tragic or comic, expected by his readers, in favor of endings ambiguous and sometimes ironic. Such an ending has three phases. First, there is an associative act, in which one character moves or gestures toward another in an act of agreement or reconciliation: In "Hills," after threatening to scream, the woman smiles at the man as he moves their baggage across the platform, reminding him to come back to finish his beer. This conciliatory movement is followed by a reaction that dissociates the character, an act of disagreement or exclusion: The man moves the bags but stops inside the barroom to have a quick drink of Anis. Finally there is some act or dialogue that brings the two previous acts together. This third element usually predicts the characters' future or comments on their final moments together: The pregnant woman, still smiling, says she is fine, which seems on the surface to bring their disagreement to a close but also suggests to the reader that she has changed in the course of the argument.

Envoi

Following my practicum, the reader will discover four very different and challenging essays which I hope will open Hemingway's fiction for you in new ways. The contributors and I have spent more time than usual with the essays, revising and honing. If you disagree with any of these essays, our efforts will be rewarded, for disagreement will push you to respond. I hope you find at least one or two of the essays exciting. As you read them, remember that Hemingway was always exploring the limits of his genre, pushing the envelope, testing traditional maxims. His experimentation with the short story, beginning in 1922, did not end until "Snows of Kilimanjaro" in 1936. In that amazing story, he wrote a novel, omitting everything but its conclusion, and inside that mini-novel he interlarded a collection of vignettes, themselves the germs of unwritten stories. There were stories written after "Snows," but the experimentation had reached its limits.

"Snows" was not the very end, however, for there remained Hemingway's experience of 17 April 1938 at a bridge across the Ebro River when the Loyalist cause in the Spanish Civil War was all but lost. At the bridgehead, Hemingway met an old Spaniard wearing steel spectacles that resembled his own. Looking at this curious reflection of himself, he clearly saw the look of final resignation in the old man's face. Without politics, the seventy-six-year-old man explained that he was a keeper of animals: goats, a cat, some pigeons. "I have come twelve kilometers now," he says, "and I think now I can go no further." The narrator urges him to his feet, but the effort is too much; the old man "sat down backwards in the dust." With the narrator's final comment, Hemingway returns to his signature ending:

> It was Easter Sunday and the Fascists were advancing toward the Ebro. It was a gray overcast day with a low ceiling so their planes were not up. That and the fact that cats know how to look after themselves was all the good luck that old man would ever have. (*Complete Stories* 58)

Hemingway left his secret sharer at the bridge – there was nothing he could do – drove on to Barcelona and turned the incident into the last of his *First Forty-Nine Stories*. In his momentary identification with that bespectacled old man, resigned to his fate but worrying about the care of his animals, Hemingway saw and recorded the end of fifteen brilliant years of short stories.

There was much more I wanted to tell you, but like that old man at the Ebro bridge, I can go no further. I too am sitting in the dust, having quite literally run out of time and space. By the time you read these words, I will have stepped into that undiscovered country beyond your reach, changing tenses as it were. This essay is my last challenge to you, my practical reader, to be always open to possibilities, to remain humble enough to trust the story, and to remain skeptical enough to think for yourself. So with no more ado, I bid you adieu, having enjoyed my pursuit as a Hemingway scholar more than it is given to most men to experience. Good night, gentlemen. Good night, sweet ladies. Good night, good night.

NOTES

1. For an overview of critical studies on "One Reader Writes" see Smith, *A Reader's Guide* 299–300.

WORKS CITED

Hemingway, Ernest. *The Complete Short Stories of Ernest Hemingway.* New York: Charles Scribner's Sons, 1987.

Ernest Hemingway Selected Letters. Ed., Carlos Baker. New York: Charles Scribner's Sons, 1981.

Green Hills of Africa. New York: Charles Scribner's Sons, 1935.

A Moveable Feast. New York: Charles Scribner's Sons, 1964.

The Nick Adams Stories. New York: Charles Scribner's Sons, 1972.

Huxley, Aldous. "Foreheads Villainous Low." *Music at Night and Other Essays.* London: Chatto & Windus, 1931.

Lawrence, D. H. *Studies in Classic American Literature.* London: Seltzer, 1923.

Lewis, Wyndham. "The Dumb Ox: A Study of Ernest Hemingway." *Life and Letters* 10 (April 1934):33–45.

Plimpton, George. "The Art of Fiction: Ernest Hemingway." *The Paris Review* 5 (Spring 1958).

Smith, Paul. *A Reader's Guide to the Short Stories of Ernest Hemingway.* Boston: G. K. Hall, 1989.

2

Reading "Up in Michigan"

NANCY R. COMLEY AND ROBERT SCHOLES

A First Reading

In this essay we discuss reading in general and reading Ernest Hemingway in particular, citing a single short story that Hemingway wrote early in his career: "Up in Michigan." Our goal is not to produce a single "right" or ultimate reading of this story, but to explore possible ways of reading it and the implications of those ways. We argue, inevitably, that certain ways of reading are better than others, in that they provide more pleasure for the reader or produce more interesting and persuasive readings. In doing this, we assume that our reader has access to a copy of the story and can number the paragraphs. Any number in square brackets, without any other indication, will refer to a paragraph in "Up in Michigan."

In many ways, this is a simple story about a couple and their first "date," which leads to a sexual encounter over the woman's protests. "Aha," you say, "date rape." "Well," we say, "yes – and no, or, perhaps, maybe." The first point we want to make about reading is that this kind of move, from a summary of the events of the story to an expression like "date rape," is one of the things we do when we read. We turn events – in this particular narrative, a sexual act – into interpretive and evaluative categories, like date rape. Such categories enable us to get control of a story, to fit it into our own thinking. We can't do without them, but they can limit us by closing down interpretive possibilities too quickly, oversimplifying something that may be more subtle and more complex than the categories we apply. Reading fictions like this is partly a matter of developing categories that are less simple and rigid.

Let's begin reading. We move through the story rapidly once, pointing out questions and problems. Then we come back and see what kinds of answers and solutions we can produce.

The first thing to read is the title. It gives us a place, Michigan, but not a time. And it offers an intriguing preposition, "Up." This probably refers to the part of Michigan in which the events of the story take place, but it may have other meanings as well. In the first two paragraphs we are introduced to two characters, Jim Gilmore and Liz Coates (as well as Mrs. Smith). The writing is very simple and direct: Jim "came," he "bought," he "was," and he "lived" [1]. The second paragraph begins by telling us about Liz, but ends by telling us how Jim reacted to her: he "liked her face" but "never thought about her" [2]. The person telling us this story (the narrator) knows – and reports – what Jim was and was not thinking and feeling, that is, he (so-called for convenience) occasionally gives us things from Jim's point of view.

The narrator also gives us things from the viewpoint of Liz, starting with the first sentence in paragraph [3]. But something else happens in this paragraph that should attract the careful reader's attention. Instead of saying, "She liked the way he walked" he says, "She liked *it* the way he walked," and continues using that construction repetitiously for most of this paragraph. Why does he do that? What's going on here? We come back to these questions but for the moment it is enough to notice that there's something odd in this use of the word "it."

The next paragraph is purely descriptive, letting us know that we are in a relatively remote and rural part of the world. Paragraph [5] opens with description, too, and the rhythm of the sentences becomes more noticeable as the narrator describes the beauty of the scene. He first puts the reader in the scene, using the second person – "From Smith's back door *you* could see" – and then puts Liz in the same place – "From Smith's back door *Liz* could see" [5]. This alignment of viewpoints is quite literal – both Liz and "you" seeing the same thing from the same place, but it is also metaphorical, bringing the reader into line with Liz's thoughts and feelings, which become the topic in the next paragraph.

20

Paragraph [6] not only tells us what Liz is thinking about at a particular time, it also uses a different tense and a different kind of narrative time. The first sentence does not say "Liz thought" but "All the time now Liz *was thinking*" (our emphasis). This use of the "iterative" mode of narration enables a writer to tell us once something that happens many times (in this case "All the time"). Here, it has the effect of emphasizing Liz's preoccupation with Jim Coates – who doesn't "seem to notice her much." We are getting our information mainly from Liz's point of view here, as we will throughout most of this narrative. For reasons we will want to think about, Hemingway has decided to present this story from that angle. We also get some other useful information in this paragraph. Jim talks about James G. Blaine, the "plumed Knight" of the Republican party, a senator and diplomat who ran for President in 1884 and was much in the news that year. This gives us a fairly persuasive way of dating these events, though the date might be earlier, because Blaine had been in the news before. This paragraph is mainly informational, telling us things we need to know about the situation of the story.

Paragraph [7] continues and intensifies the internal focus on Liz's feelings, giving us plenty of clues to her emotional state. She misses him badly, has trouble sleeping, but discovers that it is "fun to think about him too." She feels "weak and sort of sick inside" when she sees Jim coming back from his trip. These are signs of what Liz (and we) would probably call "love" – a condition the story is going to ask us to think about. Then the men come back with their load of dead deer and their new growths of beard. The big event narrated in this paragraph is something that doesn't happen: "Liz hadn't known just what would happen when Jim got back but she was sure it would be something. Nothing had happened." It is worth noting that Hemingway's narrative voice tells us nothing about how Liz reacted to this "nothing." We, too, expect something, given the way we have been told about her feelings early in this paragraph, and we, too, get nothing. As he does so often, Hemingway expects us to fill in the gaps of his narrative, to make the story our own. We must supply her feelings of disappointment, which makes them both

21

stronger and less sentimental than they would be if the author had insisted on telling us about them.

The next dozen paragraphs [8–20] are mainly conversation about the deer the men have killed on their hunting trip and information about drinking from the whiskey jug. Jim, in particular, has a big drink straight out of the jug while bringing it in, slopping some of it down his shirt front – which may be a hint that this is not his first drink of the day. During the conversation about hunting and drinking they also have at least two more "big shots." This conversation is reported without any commentary, not even a "he said" or any identification of who says what. It is generic man talk, and Hemingway gives it to us generically.

Paragraph 21 shifts back from the external reported conversation to telling us, first, about Jim's feelings, and, later, about Liz's. Jim "began to feel great" and "loved the taste and feel of the whiskey." After a dinner where the men were "feeling hilarious but acting very respectable" they talk in the front room. (Do they continue drinking? We don't know.) And Liz sits in the kitchen, pretending to read a book, waiting to see Jim so she can "take the way he looked up to bed with her." Clearly, she has a bad case of love, so bad that she wants to take Jim's image to bed with her, though what she will do with it there is one of the things we are not told.

She is in this state, "thinking about him hard" [22], when Jim comes into the kitchen, stands behind her, and puts "his arms around her." It is clear from the context that his hands are on her breasts. "Her breasts felt plump and firm and the nipples were erect under his hands" – Jim's viewpoint, we are told what he is feeling. Liz is frightened. She has never been touched this way before, but she thinks, in terms of her notion of love, "He's come to me finally. He's really come." It is worth noting that this description of an embrace is expressed in the language of coition, from the "hard" of Liz's thoughts, to her "erect" nipples, to "He's come." Hemingway charges this moment with even more sexuality than the event calls for.

The next paragraph is anchored in Liz's point of view and continues the process of using the most sexual words in the least obvious places. Liz holds herself "stiff" but when she feels Jim's erection through the back of the chair we are told only that she feels "Jim." That is, we, the readers, have to ask ourselves what part of Jim she would feel through the back of the chair and supply that in order to visualize this scene properly. We must also solve another little interpretive puzzle. We are told in no uncertain terms that, when Jim "held her tight hard" against the back of the chair, "she wanted it now." What, we must ask, is the "it," that she wanted? This is not the last of the "its" the reader must deal with, so, let us leave the interpretive question open for the moment. The paragraph ends with Jim inviting her in a whisper to "Come on for a walk."

Paragraph [24] describes their walk down the sandy road to the dock. What follows is seen mainly from Liz's perspective. We are told that, though the weather is cold, she is "hot all over from being with Jim." Jim is reduced, in this paragraph, to a pair of hands: one inside her dress, stroking her breast, the other moving from her lap to sliding up her leg. In the next two paragraphs of dialogue, Liz tells Jim "Don't" and "You mustn't." Then comes the crucial paragraph [27]:

The boards were hard. Jim had her dress up and was trying to do something to her. She was frightened but she wanted it. She had to have it but it frightened her.

The key words in this paragraph are "something" and "it." We, knowing readers that we are, know what Jim is trying to do. Liz either does not know exactly or will not allow herself to think clearly about it. "Something" looks like a vague word, but it is used precisely here because of its vagueness. And that pronoun "it" also poses an interpretive problem. In this paragraph, "it" seems to refer grammatically to "something." We are told unmistakably that "it" frightens her but that she has to have "it." Vagueness upon vagueness. Readers of this story must interpret. The text forces us to contribute to the construction of the event and its interpretation.

In paragraph [28] Liz tells Jim he mustn't do "it" and in the next Jim says "I got to. I'm going to. You know we got to." This is brief, but the shift in pronouns raises the question of whether Jim is doing something here or both Jim and Liz ("we") are doing

23

it. Jim's words also raise the interpretive question of whether Liz knows what they are doing and that they have to do it. Either he thinks she knows this, or he is trying to persuade her that she knows it.

In paragraph [30] Liz replies that they don't have to. She then says, "Oh, it isn't right. Oh, it's so big and it hurts so. You can't. Oh, Jim. Jim. Oh." Once again, the pronouns are interesting. "It" in the first of these sentences refers to what Jim is doing. In the second sentence, however, "it" refers to what Jim is doing it with. The exclamations are also interesting. Suddenly all those "Ohs." Hemingway avoids any graphic description of this sexual act, but the thrusts of Jim's body are recorded in Liz's exclamations: "Oh. . . .Oh. . . .Oh. . . .Oh." And the deed is done. There is apparently a brief lapse of time between this paragraph and the next.

We are still seeing things through the eyes of Liz in paragraph [31] but the narrator sticks to physical information, avoiding any direct statements about what she is feeling emotionally until after she starts to cry. We might call this semi-detached narration. We learn that Jim has fallen asleep on top of her and that she can't wake him. We also learn that he has hurt her. When she can't wake him up, she works her way out from under him (instead of just pushing him off) and tries to compose her clothing and hair. Then she leans over and kisses him on the cheek. He rolls over and she starts to cry. In the mist coming up from the bay "she was cold and miserable and everything felt gone."

In the closing paragraphs she tries again, unsuccessfully, to wake Jim, covers him with her coat and tucks him in, and walks up the sandy road to go to bed with that "cold mist" "coming up through the woods from the bay." We are left with some questions. Why does she kiss him and tuck him in like a baby? Why does she want to wake him up? What would he say if he awoke? What will Liz's life be like from now on?

Looking at the Scholarship

Scholarship includes such activities as establishing the accuracy of a text; determining sources of textual material; reviewing the

24

social and intellectual history of the time the text was written, and verifying authorship. A scholarly investigation can start with the question, How did the story come about? Why, for example, did this particular material interest Hemingway? One approach involves the study of manuscripts, for an analysis of a writer's drafts and revisions can give some insight into the composition of a story. We are fortunate in that many of Hemingway's manuscripts are available for study, and they show us, more often than not, that he was his own best editor.

"Up in Michigan" is one of Hemingway's earliest successful stories. It was written before he went to Paris in 1921, and may even have been drafted on location, as it were, in Petoskey, Michigan, a few miles north of Hortons Bay. In Hemingway's case, it's generally considered that almost all the stories that make up his best known early book, *In Our Time*, were written in Paris. "Up in Michigan" could not be included in that text because of its subject matter (notably the scene on the dock). The story differs from the *In Our Time* stories in that much of it is told from a woman's point of view, an issue we discuss when we talk about interpretation. But we might think of this difference as a link with some of the texts that preceded it. Shortly before he wrote "Up in Michigan," Hemingway wrote a series of sketches called "Cross Roads – An Anthology," about the different kinds of people living in a small Michigan town. These sketches were rejected by editors, but they are of interest to Hemingway scholars because they represent strong examples of Hemingway's apprentice work, showing his use of local American material. Hemingway was eager to be published in *The Saturday Evening Post*, a magazine of wide circulation which paid well for the fiction it published. Hemingway had read in that magazine a series of small-town sketches by E. W. Howe, from his "Anthology of Another Town," and they inspired "Cross Roads." How do we know this? Michael Reynolds, in his research for a Hemingway biography, found this information in the letters William B. Smith, a good friend of Hemingway's and also a writer, wrote to Hemingway. Smith and Hemingway were plotting to emulate Howe and get their work published in *The Saturday Evening Post*. Neither one succeeded (Reynolds 96–7). However, writing the

"Cross Roads" sketches gave Hemingway practice in presenting characters and situations with a minimum of detail. One of the sketches, "Pauline Snow," has been cited as a precursor to "Up in Michigan." It concerns a "beautiful girl," courted by a crude fellow named Art, who is favored by her guardian. Here are the concluding paragraphs, in which Pauline's situation might be compared to that of Liz Coates in "Up in Michigan":

> Pauline's big eyes would look frightened – but she went off with him in the dusk along the road. There was a red line of afterglow along the hills toward Charlevoix, and Pauline said to Art, "Don't you think that's awfully pretty, Art?"
>
> "We didn't come here to talk about sunsets, kiddo!" said Art, and put his arm around her.
>
> After a while some of the neighbors made a complaint, and they sent Pauline away to the correction school down at Coldwater. Art was away for awhile, and then came back and married one of the Jenkins girls. (Griffin 1985, 124)

Some critics might call the sketches "derivative": that is, they seem to echo Howe's style rather than asserting Hemingway's. Howe's "Anthology" had itself been preceded by Edgar Lee Masters' best-selling *Spoon River Anthology* in 1915, which features a group of poetic monologues about their lives spoken by the dead in a small midwestern cemetery. At this stage in his writing career, however, Hemingway's style was still developing. We can see in his early work an attempt to emulate a popular magazine style and genre, but present, too, are hallmarks of his later style. For example, his presentation of the differences in perception between men and women: Pauline is struck by the beauty of nature; Art is blinded by his hormones. Here, too, we have the question of influence: How do writers come to write the way they do? Do they learn by imitation, by borrowing, or, do they, as T. S. Eliot says of mature writers, steal from other writers? In his autobiographical book, *A Moveable Feast,* Hemingway has a chapter titled "Miss Stein Instructs" in which he gives some credit to Gertrude Stein for advice and instruction on writing and painting. Critics like to point out that Hemingway learned a lot about the use of repetition from Stein, who uses much repetition in

26

her work, and the repetition of "she liked" in "Up in Michigan" has been attributed to Stein's influence. But Hemingway's story was written before he met Stein (who, when she did read it, did not think the story was publishable). Hemingway certainly did read Stein's work after he went to Paris, and it's likely he did learn from her more about the effective use of repetition, but we can see in paragraph [3] of "Up in Michigan" that he already had a sense of its usefulness and force. Each "liked" builds in intensity on the preceding one, so that the final "liking," as an ongoing condition, is very strong indeed. Sherwood Anderson's *Winesburg, Ohio* (1919) is also cited as an influence on "Up in Michigan" and "Cross Roads," because Anderson's work presents small town midwestern lives with a new form of realism, based in an oral tradition. But we know from Reynolds' work that Hemingway drafted "Up in Michigan" before reading *Winesburg, Ohio*, a book that, when he did read it, he indeed admired.

There are three typescript versions of "Up in Michigan" in the Hemingway Collection at the John F. Kennedy Library in Boston. They give us some insight into Hemingway's processes of composition and revision. In the earliest version, these first four lines are crossed out:

Wesley Dilworth got the dimple in his chin from his mother. Her name had been Liz Buell. Jim Dilworth married her when he came to Horton's Bay from Canada and bought the mill with A. J. Stroud. (Kennedy Library/EH 800; Smith 163–77)

This version of the story might have answered the question, Where and when was Wesley Dilworth conceived? This beginning, though crossed out, probably stayed in Hemingway's mind as he wrote the story, because there also exist two variant endings, one of them an incomplete description of an embarrassed Jim and Liz meeting at breakfast the next morning, and the other telling how Liz felt after leaving Jim on the dock asleep. It reads:

Liz was frightened and sick when she got up to her room. She put on one of her unwell pads because she was afraid of blood getting on the sheets. She felt ashamed and sick and cried and prayed until she fell

27

asleep. She woke up frightened and stiff and aching. "What if I have a baby?" she thought. It was the first time she thought about it. It really was. She was so frightened the sweat ran down under her armpits . . . she was too frighted [sic] to cry. She thought about having a baby until it was morning. (Smith 168)

Paul Smith, on whose study of the manuscripts we are drawing, comments: "That tentative beginning and its associated ending show the signs of Hemingway's attempt to break into the market for popular fiction from the fall of 1919 through the summer of 1920" (168). How Wesley got his dimple would have been a beginning with popular appeal, suitable for a magazine like *The Saturday Evening Post,* but the story quickly took a different turn, from a light story of a country courtship toward its final rougher nature. We can see from the excised ending just how frightened and hurt Liz was, and we should ask why Hemingway felt the story didn't need this ending. That beginning and those endings were gone a few months later, when the second typescript, with Hemingway's Paris address in 1922, was completed. "Up in Michigan" was first published in *Three Stories and Ten Poems* (1923) in a small press edition in Paris. The two other stories were "My Old Man" and "Out of Season," both of which were subsequently included in *In Our Time* in 1925. "Up in Michigan" was also supposed to appear in that collection, but the editors at Boni and Liveright, the publisher, considered it too sexually explicit for American readers. When *In Our Time* was reissued by Scribner's in 1930, Hemingway tried to tone down the sexual material to make the story publishable. The third typescript manuscript, in which he tried to rewrite the scene on the dock, shows how futile his attempts were. As he wrote to his editor, Maxwell Perkins, his attempt to keep the story "from being libelous . . . takes all its character away" (*Selected Letters* 326). Hemingway's concern was not simply with the sexual scenes, but that he had based the story on the actions, both real and imagined, of real people. In the version finally published in America, he used fictitious names. As late as 1938, when Hemingway was putting together a collection of his first forty-nine stories, his editor again balked at the sexual explicitness of "Up in Michigan," and asked Hemingway to cut some lines. In refusing to do so, Hemingway wrote to Perkins:

It is an important story in my work. . . . It is not dirty but is very sad. I did not write so well then, especially dialogue. But there on the dock it got suddenly absolutely right and it is the point of the whole story and the beginning of all the naturalness I ever got. (*Selected Letters* 468)

Although Hemingway does not elaborate on why "Up in Michigan" is an "important story" in his work, this brief overview of scholarship might provide some reasons. His own comments suggest that this story constituted a breakthrough in the writing of dialogue. Hemingway had an excellent ear for dialogue, and he used it as an integral part of much of his writing.

Important, too, was Hemingway's choice of setting. "Up in Michigan" was the first of a number of stories set in a locale where Hemingway vacationed during his childhood and early manhood. The particular importance of this area of northern Michigan as a stimulus to Hemingway's imagination is evident not only in his early fiction, but also in his return to that landscape near the end of his writing career, in a story he did not complete, "The Last Good Country." A number of Hemingway scholars are interested in gathering biographical information on the Michigan phase of Hemingway's life as a means of interpreting his work. One such book is Constance Cappel Montgomery's *Hemingway in Michigan* (1966), which covers Hemingway's time there, from his first family vacation at the age of one to his marriage in Horton Bay in 1921 to Hadley Richardson. Such scholarship also seeks to answer the question, Where did Hemingway get the material for his stories? Montgomery finds that Hemingway's descriptions of the town are "photographically accurate." The events concerning Liz and Jim pose more of a problem, and Montgomery avoids it. (Residents of Horton Bay have suggested that the young Hemingway himself had a tryst on the dock with an older waitress – and, just for the record, the real Wesley Dilworth, a boyhood friend of Hemingway's, was conceived four years after his parents, Elizabeth Buell and James Dilworth, were married [Baker 574, 567].)

Montgomery is primarily interested in Hemingway as a

reporter: "Hemingway's descriptions are those of a reporter who saw the landscape accurately and without sentiment" (126), she writes, and "In 'Up in Michigan,' Hemingway wrote certainly about what he knew and about 'the people and the places and how the weather was'" (127, quoting Hemingway). Montgomery is a reader who likes her fiction to be "real," as one can see from the value she places on accurate and objective reporting. Whether anyone's vision or writing can be truly objective is an interesting question, one we touch on as we go along.

Much of Hemingway's fiction is read as if it were autobiographical. For example, at least two of Hemingway's biographers (Meyers 49; Lynn 108) want the events on the dock in "Up in Michigan" to be the scenario for Hemingway's sexual initiation, over which a cloud of obscurity hangs. In the stories of *In Our Time*, although we can say that Nick Adams and Harold Krebs are surrogates for Hemingway, they are not Hemingway. In the excised ending of "Big Two-Hearted River," published in *The Nick Adams Stories* as "On Writing," Hemingway/Nick wrote, "The only writing that was any good was what you made up, what you imagined. That made everything come true. . . . Nick in the stories was never himself. He made him up" (237, 238). Note Hemingway's use of "true" (one of his favorite words): He doesn't mean "real." Much of Hemingway's writing is generated by events he experienced. Writers often write about what they know about, but good writers don't report, they transform events when they construct a fiction. If a writer is talented enough, his fiction rings true: It sounds "real."

Let us look at "A Very Short Story" as an example of the transformation of something that happened to Hemingway. Here are the biographical facts: At the age of nineteen, Hemingway, who had volunteered as an American Red Cross ambulance driver for the Italian army, was wounded. In the army hospital in Milan, he met twenty-six-year old Agnes von Kurowsky, an American Red Cross nurse, and he fell in love with her. Their pet names for one another were "Kid" and "Mrs. Kid." When she volunteered for service in Florence during an influenza epidemic, he wrote to her daily, and sometimes twice a day. She wrote him when she could find the time, and when another epidemic broke out in Treviso, she went there. His wounds prevented him from returning to his Red Cross duties, so he traveled a bit in Italy, and saw her several more times before returning to the United States. In the meantime, he had written to friends and family about Ag, as he called her, saying he intended to marry her, and that he was coming home to get a job that would support them both. It should be noted, especially when comparing the fiction ("A Very Short Story") to the writer's life, that (according to Agnes von Kurowsky herself) their relationship was never sexually consummated (Villard).

When Hemingway arrived home, he partied with his friends, and had not found a job by March of 1919, when a letter arrived from Italy to say that Agnes had met an Italian lieutenant and planned to marry him. According to Hemingway's older sister, Marcelline, this rejection made him physically ill for several days. A few months later, von Kurowsky wrote to say that the family of her Italian lieutenant, who were members of the Italian nobility, had forbidden him to marry her, and that Hemingway should feel revenged. That Hemingway's anger and bitterness remained for some time after these events is evident in the tone of "A Very Short Story," to which we now turn as an example of Hemingway's transformation of personal experience.

Here, too, we can learn something from the manuscript versions of the story. Originally, it was written in the first person, the nurse was named "Ag," and the story began, "One hot evening in Milan they carried me up onto the roof." Realizing that the story might be considered libelous, Milan was changed to Padua, Ag became Luz, and I became he. We also note that contrasting sexual encounters have been added to the story: Nurse and patient make love in a hospital bed, and after the jilting, carnality in a taxicab represents a degradation of love. In the story, the young man returns to the front; he's obviously a soldier, not a Red Cross volunteer. Why was it necessary for the writer to make his young man a soldier at the front, with his nurse-lover back at the hospital writing him many letters? The real life situations have been reversed, to make the young man appear more of a hero. Whose side is the story on? We need hardly ask, for our writer has constructed characters with well-defined traits: This soldier holds "tight on to himself so he would not blab about anything during the silly talky time" under anesthesia. Not blabbing is a key male trait in this story. And Luz? Look at the fourth paragraph of the story. She writes a lot. And how does she write? Look at the way she's paraphrased: "and how much she loved him and how it was impossible to get along without him and how terrible it was missing him at night." We note her use of exaggeration and hyperbole, the repetition of "and how" that suggests a loosely constructed prose style and what's worse, a "talky" one. Go back to the second paragraph of the story, and the "friend or enema" joke. Luz is the giver of the enema, the one who loosens things up, the one who flushes, literally and figuratively. In the fifth paragraph, it's quite clear that Luz sets the rules of what the young man is and is not to do. And in the sixth, the penultimate paragraph, note the paraphrase of Luz's letter: hyperbole again, and repetition. Especially noticeable: her reference to their love as a "boy and girl affair." She has reduced those passionate nights in the hospital bed to what sounds like puppy love. The young man's anger and pain are packed into the denial of Luz twice and forever: "The major did not marry her in the spring, or any other time," and she "never got an answer to the letter to Chicago about it." The final negation is his degradation of the act of love.

The young man is the one we're supposed to feel sorry for, because his values are privileged in the story. He's the one who doesn't talk too much or write too much; he holds on to himself, and is the one who most wants to make their relationship "so they could not lose it." Hemingway's art lies in his ability to present these two characters with opposing characteristics with great economy and effect. We submit the story to only a partial interpretation here, just enough, we hope, to suggest the kind of transformation that takes place when life is transmuted into art, and just enough to show why reading Hemingway's fiction as Hemingway's life is not a good idea.

"Up in Michigan" and *In Our Time*

"Up in Michigan" would have been the first story in *In Our Time* (see the letter to Edward O'Brien, quoted below), if Hemingway's publishers had been willing to include it. When he collected his first forty-nine stories for publication in 1938, he put "Up in Michigan" in front of the first story from *In Our Time*, with the other stories from that volume following in their original order. Because of this history, it makes sense to see "Up in Michigan" as belonging to that collection – or perhaps as a prelude to that collection, as it is not set in "our" time – that is Hemingway's time – but a generation earlier. Before returning to the interpretive questions raised in the first section of this essay, we consider, in the present section, some aspects of the whole collection, *In Our Time*, as it relates to "Up In Michigan."

The title of this volume, like the title of Hemingway's first novel, *The Sun Also Rises*, comes from a religious text – in this case from the Episcopalian *Book of Common Prayer*. In the prayer the speaker asks the Lord for "peace in our time" – a phrase given added irony long after Hemingway used it, when the British statesman Neville Chamberlain claimed to have reached an accommodation with Hitler and thus to have brought about "peace in our time" just before the Second World War broke out. But Hemingway was already using the title ironically in 1925. Many of the stories and interchapters in *In Our Time* are about war and others have undertones and overtones of violence. Five years after the first publication of *In Our Time*, a second edition came out with one story added and put at the front of the book as a kind of introduction. That story is "On the Quai at Smyrna," in which, through the voice of a British naval officer involved in evacuating refugees in the Greco-Turkish war, we learn of women dying on the quai and others having babies there and in the hold of the evacuating ship: "They had them all right. You just covered them over with something and let them go at it" (*Complete Stories* 64). Others apparently were still holding dead babies in their arms.

"On the Quai at Smyrna" was titled "Introduction by the

33

Author" and put at the beginning of the collection in 1930. In the 1938 publication of *The Fifth Column and the First Forty-nine Stories,* "Up in Michigan" was put ahead of it. The next full-length story in the collection (after the short interchapter 1), is "Indian Camp." Let us think about these three stories as a sequence for a moment: "Up in Michigan," "On the Quai at Smyrna," and "Indian Camp." The central event in "Up in Michigan" combines sex and violence and takes place on a dock in the dark. It ends with Liz covering Jim up with her coat. A "quai" is, of course, a dock, but made of stone. In "On the Quai at Smyrna" the central images are of violence and childbirth. The next story, "Indian Camp," is about a birth by Caesarean section without anesthetic. It ends with the suicide of the husband, who has been unable to endure his wife's screams of pain, and young Nick Adams' reaction to the whole event. In the final scene Nick's father is rowing away from the carnage at sunrise, while Nick trails his hand in the warm water and thinks about birth and death, feeling sure that he will never die.

We offer these crude summaries as an indication of how intricately Hemingway has interlaced the themes and images in these stories: sex, birth, death, and violence, with a strong maternal theme running through all of them. The maternal theme in "On the Quai at Smyrna" and "Indian Camp" helps us to see the maternal quality of Liz's gesture of tucking Jim in with her coat, just as the women with their dead babies offer an ironic echo of Liz trying to wake her insensible consort. These echoes – harmonies and dissonances – give Hemingway's apparently simple stories an astonishing richness for a careful and thoughtful reader. They reward such reading so powerfully that it becomes almost inescapable. If we let him, Hemingway will teach us how to read. The stories also resist interpretive simplification. They are very clear, but they are also enigmatic, with meanings that spread out in ripples from their apparently simple core. To read, to visualize, to participate actively in the creation of the story – and to follow threads of meaning without moving too quickly toward closure – these are the lessons we can learn from a serious engagement with Hemingway's short fiction, beginning with a story like "Up in Michigan" that he completed at the age of twenty-two.

In "Indian Camp," across the lake in Michigan, a woman's body is again the scene of a violent assault – but in the name of medicine. A crude Caesarean is performed without anesthetic in order to save the lives of an Indian mother and her baby. The doctor says to his young son Nick, "her screams are not important. I don't hear them because they are not important" (*Complete Stories* 68). As it turns out, her screams are important: The woman's husband, trapped in his bunk with a wounded foot, cannot stand them and slits his throat. Thus Nick, who witnesses both birth and death, learns some harsh lessons. He may not at his age realize that the price of sex is often pregnancy, but he has seen death connected with birth. The one who gives birth does not die, however. It is the father who dies, because, according to Nick's father, "he couldn't stand things." Fathers are the ones who, in Dr. Adams' terms, are "the worst sufferers in these little affairs" (69).

As we consider the other stories in what Paul Smith (borrowing a term from the traditional interpretation of Chaucer's "Canterbury Tales") has called the "marriage group" of *In Our Time*, we can see that "Up in Michigan" offers the first statement of the themes of sex and marriage, which "Indian Camp" continues. The next full story, "The Doctor and the Doctor's Wife," continues this marriage theme, even as it continues Nick's education about married life. Though Nick does not see the confrontation between his father and the Indian, Dick Boulton, or hear the ensuing conversation between his mother and father, his side in their dispute is made clear in the few words he speaks at the end of the story. They come after the doctor has undergone two scenes of emasculation.

When Dick arrives to cut up some logs he refers to them as "stolen," and further angers Nick's father by trimming his title to "Doc." Angered, the doctor threatens to punch Boulton, but both know that the bigger, stronger Indian could easily beat the doctor, who turns away in frustration and goes to his room in the cottage. There, he has an equally frustrating conversation with his wife, who is lying in her darkened room with her Bible and her Christian Science journals nearby. She just cannot believe that Dick Boulton would deliberately start an argument to get out of the work he owes the doctor. This frustrating conversation takes place between their two rooms – she with her Christian texts around her, and he, compulsively loading and ejecting shells from his shotgun and then carefully cleaning it with a rag. The doctor's gun in this onanistic ritual is clearly a phallic image. In loading and ejecting instead of firing, he enacts a parodic version of impotence and frustration.

He is frustrated by his inability to stand up to Boulton and by his failure to communicate with his wife. As he leaves, slamming the door in his fury, his wife tells him to send Nick in to her. Nick is in the hemlock woods (as Liz was on the hemlock planks of the dock), reading, when his father delivers the maternal message. Nick tells his father where some squirrels (for hunting) may be found and says simply, "I want to go with you." Though Nick hasn't seen the two little episodes that we have, he has absorbed enough of the marital tensions in the household to know that he must choose. And he chooses the woods. As a group these "marriage" stories explore the difficulty of communicating across the gender gap, or what Hemingway's contemporary James Thurber called "The War between Men and Women." The topic is introduced in "Up in Michigan," where Liz and Joe have such different notions of what their relationship entails. This theme continues in the next two stories.

In "The End of Something" we are still up in Michigan and by now Nick is a teenager. What is the "something" that is at an end? The opening of the story, describing Hortons Bay as it was in the old days and is now, suggests that one thing that has ended is the life of Hortons Bay as a lumbering town. One function of this opening description of the broken pieces of the former mill is to show how it is perceived by Nick and his girlfriend Marjorie as they row by it, trolling for trout:

"There's our old ruin, Nick" Marjorie said.
Nick, rowing, looked at the white stone in the green trees. (*Complete Stories* 79)

Marjorie romanticizes the mill site as an "old ruin," marking it as a shared vision. But Nick's gaze abstracts salient objects and primary colors from the landscape. In the full context of the story, because we know Nick has planned to break up with Marjorie, we can see his refusal to romanticize as a form of resistance to Marjorie herself. Hemingway's male characters in these stories (and in such a later collection as *Men without Women*) often retreat into abstraction when confronted with the more romantic and imaginative visions of his women. In "Hills Like White Elephants" from that later volume, for instance, the woman is pregnant and the man wants her to have an abortion, but he never mentions these words. Losing it – the baby, the creative vision, the relationship – is what the story is about.

In "Up in Michigan" this kind of difference between masculine and feminine readings of the text of human sexuality is very evident. Liz's romantic expectations are clear in the phrases that express her reaction to Jim's first touch: "He's come to me finally. He's really come" (61). Encoded here is a sexual innuendo (of which Liz is undoubtedly innocent). There are echoes of romantic songs and stories in which the good girl need only sit and wait until her Prince Charming comes along. These romantic expectations contrast powerfully with the actuality of Jim's inebriated gropings and thrustings.

"The End of Something" is later in time (around 1914, say) but earlier in the lives of its characters. It is a story of adolescence, of a summer romance at a time of life when being in love is supposed to be "fun" – but for Nick it isn't fun any more. Why? Nick is not happy – or says he is not – that Marjorie knows "everything." We see that she loves to fish, does it well, and handles a boat well, too. It seems that Nick has taught her these things and she has apparently learned too well. If Marjorie now knows too much, Nick apparently knows – or wants to know – less and less. He keeps saying, "I don't know," when she asks what is wrong. Finally, at the sight of "the moon, coming over the hills," which should be the cue for a romantic moment, Nick can only blurt out, "It isn't fun anymore." Hemingway's young male characters are deeply invested in "fun." His women seem to want something else, something romantic, which colors their perceptions of the reality in which they find themselves. Like Liz, they often seem both more romantic and more mature than the boy/men they "love." In the gap between these two gendered perspectives many of Hemingway's best stories are situated.

What Nick calls "it," Marjorie calls "love." "Isn't love any fun?" (81), she asks. But neither the noun nor the pronoun may do justice to what these two adolescents were experiencing. Nick, however, accepts Marjorie's word for it and says that no, love isn't fun anymore. At Nick's negative response Marjorie leaves gracefully, rowing away in the boat. Shortly after this, Nick's buddy Bill shows up to ask, "Did she go all right?" Obviously the guys had discussed the break-up beforehand. Bill asks if they had "a scene" which suggests that he had a certain code of behavior in mind for Marjorie. As we know, however, there was no scene, and Nick tells Bill this and sends him away. Marjorie has obviously taken the "end of something" in a more dignified way than Bill expected her to, and this, among other things, must be thought of as an element in Nick's obvious remorse.

Although Hemingway insists on a significant difference in the way males and females perceive love, sex, and marriage, he is usually far from endorsing the perceptions and values of either gender. Above all, as "Up in Michigan" so plainly demonstrates, he is no simple apologist for male attitudes or behavior in these matters.

The next story in *In Our Time*, "The Three-Day Blow," is a sequel that occurs shortly after the events narrated in "The End of Something." In this story Nick and Bill get drunk during an autumn storm and discuss baseball, books, and finally, "That Marge business," as Bill puts it. Not only is Bill anti-marriage – "Once a man's married he's absolutely bitched" – but we find that he disapproves of Marjorie because of her background: "You can't mix oil and water and you can't mix that sort of thing any more than if I'd marry Ida that works for Strattons" (91). It's a class issue for Bill, who says that now Marjorie can marry "somebody of her own sort." Nick, however, still feels remorse, until he has enough liquor in him to feel optimistic again: "Nothing was finished. Nothing was ever lost. . . . There was always a way

38

out" (92). Outside, still high but clear-headed, Nick feels as if the three-day blow has blown away "that Marge business"; his remorse is gone with the wind.

We do not intend to lead our readers through every story in *In Our Time*, but just to indicate how "Up in Michigan," placed where Hemingway placed it in his own story collection, serves to introduce themes played in other keys throughout his stories. We do, however, want to note something about the book as a whole. The arrangement of the longer stories separated by numbered "interchapters" or very short vignettes is striking and somewhat disorienting to a first reader. The interchapters are there because, at that time, Hemingway liked to work in that very short form, which is closely linked to his early journalism. (Some of the interchapters are rewritten versions of pieces first composed in the reportorial mode.) He wanted to include work in this minimal form in his first major collection of short fiction. In a letter to his editor and friend Edward O'Brien, written in September 1924, Hemingway wrote,

> I have written 14 stories and have a book ready to publish. It is to be called In Our Time and one of the chapters of the In Our Time I sent you comes in between each story. That was what I originally wrote them for, chapter headings. All the stories have a certain unity, the first 5 are in Michigan, starting with Up in Michigan, which you know and in between each one comes bang! the In Our Time. (*Selected Letters* 123)

We have explored the connecting links among the stories in *In Our Time*. Now let us briefly consider the interrupting "bang!" of the interchapters. From Hemingway's letter, it is clear that he considers the interchapters the "in our time" part of *In Our Time*. They all deal specifically with public violence: war, bullfighting, crime, political executions. They are Hemingway's way of getting the larger public world into a relationship we must see as simultaneous with the private world of the stories. With this in mind, it becomes clear that "On the Quai at Smyrna" belongs with the interchapters, as a kind of prelude to them, just as "Up in Michigan" is a prelude to the stories. And the bang of the interchapters intersects with the quieter violence of the stories.

First of all, there are some direct connections. Nick Adams is a character in at least one of the interchapters, where he sits, wounded on the Italian front, trying to have a witty conversation with the semi-conscious Rinaldi. The interchapters were first published as chapters in a limited edition called *in our time* in 1924. Two other stories that were originally chapters of the 1924 *in our time* collection were elevated to story status for the 1925 *In Our Time:* "A Very Short Story" and "The Revolutionist." "A Very Short Story" is a personal story emerging from the War, and "The Revolutionist" is a portrait of an idealistic young leftist who has been tortured in Hungary and ends up in prison in Switzerland. These two works were elevated from interchapter to story, not only because they were a bit longer than the others, but also because they take the matter of public violence in war and politics into the realm of the personal. "Our time," as Hemingway represents it, is precisely a time in which there is no refuge from the public and the violent, however much one might seek it. "Big Two-Hearted River," on the surface a fishing idyll, is also a story about the impossibility of escaping the larger issues of the time, the wars and all the physical and psychic suffering they bring with them.

No treatment of Hemingway can begin to deal with his work satisfactorily if it does not confront the role of bullfighting in his writing. In *In Our Time* there are six bullfighting interchapters that make a sequence. We believe that the importance of bullfighting for Hemingway lay in what he saw as its ability to contain and organize the public violence shaping the world of "our time." He saw bullfighting as an art (and wrote a whole book about that art, *Death in the Afternoon*) in which death and violence were not merely represented but enacted in a ritual that was both timeless and of "our time." We may or may not wish to accept his view, but, to understand him we must understand how he felt about bullfighting. The bullfighting sequence from *In Our Time* demonstrates amply that the bull is not the only creature at risk in the ring, just as the other stories and especially the interchapters demonstrate that violence and pain permeate the rest of life as well. Humans try to control this violence with art and imagination, whether it is Nick trying out a witty expression on the gravely wounded Rinaldi, or Liz tucking Jim Coates in on the dock, as if he were her child or she his nurse.

The simple, enigmatic texts of *In Our Time* invite endless interpretation as do few others that are as readable and accessible, but it is not our intention to provide readings of all the stories. That is always and finally the business of each reader. We return to "Up in Michigan" now and consider the questions of interpretation raised in our preliminary reading and the critical issues involved in trying to answer those questions.

Interpreting "Up in Michigan"

Let us start with that big, clumsy but important question that hovers over the story as we read it in our own time: Is this a story of "date rape"? In 1922 this expression was simply not in our vocabulary. Now it is unavoidable. This tells us something important about all acts of interpretation: They involve two different scenes, a scene and time of writing and a scene and time of reading. Interpretation is always to some extent a negotiation between these two scenes. One great issue is how much weight each should receive in reading any text. Should the interpretive effort be directed totally or primarily to an attempt to recover the exact intention the author may have had in producing the text? Or is the reader free to make the text mean whatever he or she wants it to mean? Let us make our own position on this matter as clear as possible. We think that recovering the author's meaning – to the extent that this is possible – is an essential part of the interpretive process. It is something we all need to learn to do – and not just with literary texts but with all sorts of messages that we encounter daily. It is also a game, with rules, that can be fun to play.

On the other hand, we also believe that no author ever can be entirely clear about his or her own intentions, nor can authors actually realize in any text all that they might intend to accomplish. Furthermore, it is also important to ask what a text means to us, here and now. And if we sense a gap between what the author may have intended and the meanings we find in a text, we must raise questions about this gap. This is one place where

41

criticism – as opposed to interpretation – can begin. But in order for it to begin, we must reach some clear view of the differences between the author's view of things and our own. Coming back to "Up in Michigan," we must ask both what Hemingway may have intended in 1922 and what we understand now. And we must raise the further question of how well the story stands up. That is, does it have anything important to say to us now, about the lives that we presently live?

The question of "date rape" can be raised in a number of ways. It can, for instance, be used simply to short circuit or shut down any careful reading of the story. Here is a man who has forced sex on a woman who said, "No" – wicked man, trivial story. Or it could be read according to some other already written interpretive script: "Women always say 'No' but mean 'Yes', so what's new?" Both of these readings, in our view, turn a subtle and complex little story into something far less interesting. To interpret the story with a subtlety that attempts to match that of the writing, we must examine carefully some decisions the au-thor has made about what we are told, and when, and how – and what we are not told, as well. Perhaps the most important of Hemingway's decisions was to tell the crucial events of the story from Liz Coates' point of view.

There might be many answers to the question of why this point of view was adopted. It might be, simply, that the story is more interesting from her viewpoint than from that of the intoxicated Jim. But it might also be that telling the story this way enabled Hemingway to give us a closer look at this charac-ter's state of mind before and during the episode on the dock. In paragraph 23, the following sentences are crucial:

She felt Jim right through the back of the chair and she couldn't stand it and then something clicked inside of her and the feeling was warmer and softer. Jim held her tight hard against the chair and she wanted it now and Jim whispered, "Come on for a walk."

As the reader turns these words into images and sensations – a vital part of the interpretive process – he or she must imagine Liz feeling the pressure of Jim's erection through the back of the chair, at first having a kind of negative reaction ("she couldn't stand it") and then a response in which her desire matches his own – something clicks inside her and she feels warmer and softer – so that when he asks her to walk out with him, she comes willingly.

In paragraph 26, we are told that Liz, as one of Jim's hands strokes her breast inside her dress and the other is in her lap, "was very frightened and didn't know how he was going to go about things but she snuggled up close to him." A few paragraphs later, when Jim is trying to do "something" to her, we are told that "She was frightened but she wanted it. She had to have it but it frightened her." All this evidence, as we interpret it, tells us that Liz is sufficiently ignorant about the mechanics of sex to be unsure of what is going to happen to her. She wants "something," but she isn't exactly sure what "it" will be or how Jim will "go about things." It is clear that Liz feels that the man is the one who will do whatever "things" are done, but the vagueness of the words "things," "something," and, of course, "it" convey to us the vagueness of Liz's own thoughts here. Whether she really "knows" and is repressing this knowledge or really "doesn't know," is open to interpretive argument, but it seems clear from Hemingway's decisions about point of view and particular words that he wants us to see Liz as saying "Yes," in many ways in response to a demand she doesn't fully understand, and then saying, "No," as the penetration she could not imagine actually occurs.

Perhaps few women of Liz's age in our own time would be quite as innocent as she seems to be, but the doubts, the indecisions, and the wanting and not wanting should not be difficult for us now, both men and women, to understand.

To finish interpreting this text, however, we must go on to the final paragraph. Liz tucks Jim in with her own coat, as if he were a sleeping child instead of a man who has just hurt her sexually. How are we to read this? Liz is miserable, crying, and cannot wake the drunken and sated man. For her, "everything felt gone." Yet she performs this loving, protective action before leaving the dock. We are inclined to read this as Liz's attempt to give a domestic or familial shape to what has happened. By treating Jim as she might treat her child or her husband, if she had one, she is trying to turn the episode into a courtship, whatever it may have been. It also shows us a person too kind to leave a man in that condition uncovered to the cold mist coming up the bay.

What, then, are we to imagine as the future of Liz and Jim? Scholarship tells us that Hemingway began writing this as a version of how the parents of a friend of his got married. From this we might imagine that Liz and Jim did move from here to marriage and family life. But the story could also have ended like the early sketch, "Pauline Snow," in which the girl is disgraced and finally has to leave the area. As with other aspects of this story, Hemingway has developed it in such a way as to leave interpretation open rather than closed. We can speculate about the future lives of this couple – and are even perhaps invited to do so – but there is no evidence here that will enable us to settle on a particular ending.

What we have is a classic confrontation between female tenderness and male sexual drive. And one of the things that is interesting about this particular version of that old story is how fully Hemingway's sympathies are enlisted on the female side of the equation, though he clearly understands how it looks from the male side as well. The prose is very clear and relatively simple, but the thoughts and feelings have a surprising subtlety and complexity. The writing is also characterized by a probity and accuracy of feeling that go deep enough to get beyond the behavioral fashions of any particular time. Hemingway's greatest achievement is to have written of his own time in a way that is meaningful for our time as well.

WORKS CITED

Baker, Carlos. *Ernest Hemingway: A Life Story.* New York: Charles Scribner's Sons, 1969.

Griffin, Peter. *Along with Youth: Hemingway the Early Years.* New York: Oxford University Press, 1985.

Hemingway, Ernest. *The Complete Short Stories of Ernest Hemingway.* New York: Charles Scribner's Sons, 1987.

"Up in Michigan"

Ernest Hemingway Selected Letters. Ed., Carlos Baker. New York: Charles Scribner's Sons, 1981.

The Nick Adams Stories. New York: Charles Scribner's Sons, 1972.

Lynn, Kenneth S. *Hemingway*. New York: Simon and Schuster, 1987.

Meyers, Jeffrey. *Hemingway: A Biography*. New York: Harper and Row, 1985.

Montgomery, Constance Cappel. *Hemingway in Michigan*. New York: Fleet, 1966.

Reynolds, Michael. *The Young Hemingway*. Oxford: Blackwell, 1986.

Smith, Paul. "Three Versions of 'Up in Michigan' 1921–1930." *Resources for American Literary Study* 15.2 (1985):163–77.

Tyler, Lisa. "Ernest Hemingway's Date Rape Story: Sexual Trauma in 'Up in Michigan.'" *The Hemingway Review* 13.2 (Spring 1994):1–11.

Villard, Henry S., and James Nagel. *Hemingway in Love and War*. Boston: Northeastern University Press, 1989.

3

"Now I Lay Me": Nick's Strange Monologue, Hemingway's Powerful Lyric, and the Reader's Disconcerting Experience

JAMES PHELAN

READING "Now I Lay Me" is a moving yet disconcerting experience. This claim makes for a succinct opening sentence, but it also raises two questions: What do I mean by "experience"? And is experience something that remains the same or varies from one reader to the next? One could write – indeed, many have written – books trying to specify the precise quality of literary experience and trying to account for the role of the reader in that experience. Since neither I nor you want me to undertake any long-winded theoretical disquisition here, I offer brief answers now and rely on my work with "Now I Lay Me" to flesh out their implications. By "experience" I mean the complex, multi-layered, part intuitive, part self-conscious responding to literature that readers do as they read. I attend to the complexity and multi-layered nature of the experience here by focusing on the interlocking processes of understanding, feeling, and judging, or what I call the cognitive, emotive, and ethical components of our reading. Because different readers bring different backgrounds, experiences, personalities, and beliefs to their reading, they will have somewhat different experiences of the same text. Nevertheless, readers frequently seek to join the author's intended audience, to become the ideal person the author implicitly addresses. It is this "authorial audience" I focus on for the better part of this essay, and it is this audience I refer to when I talk about how "we" respond to Hemingway's text.[1] When I discuss the ethical component of "Now I Lay Me," I – inevitably – also talk about my own judgments and evaluations.

Reading "Now I Lay Me" challenges our understanding because of its unusual structure and narrative technique. A small, easily resolved difficulty involves the narrator's identity: This Nick is never explicitly identified as "Nick Adams," but any reader of *In Our Time* or *Men without Women* will automatically supply the surname and the accompanying identity. A more substantial difficulty involves the story's organization. Readers have frequently commented that it splits in the middle, with the first half devoted to the range of Nick's memories during his sleepless summer and the second devoted to his memory of a conversation on one particular night. Furthermore, the narrative situation is puzzling: Nick is remembering past nights spent remembering – in other words, offering a memory of his memories or a metamemory. This situation seems linked to the story's sudden pronoun and tense shifts: from "we" to "I" in the first sentence, from past to present at several points. But perhaps the key to understanding the story's design is the relation between its lyric and its narrative elements. For the purposes of this essay, I define these genres as follows: "narrative" is the representation of a sequence of events in which a character undergoes some recognizable change – in understanding, feeling, or external circumstance – that the audience is asked to make some judgment about; "lyric" is the representation of a character (or speaker) who gives voice to a set of attitudes, thoughts, emotions, or choices that the audience is asked not to judge but to contemplate and imaginatively participate in.[2] Given these understandings, we can pose the questions about "Now I Lay Me" this way: Is Hemingway using lyric moments, for example, his evocation of Nick's fishing experiences, as part of a story about some change in Nick, either during that summer of sleepless nights or now as he tells us about that summer? Alternatively, is Hemingway using narrative sequences, such as Nick's account of his mother burning his father's things, as part of a prose lyric, one in which Hemingway reveals and explores Nick's essentially static situation?

"Now I Lay Me" is emotionally disconcerting because it contains a significant gap between the gentle resignation of Nick's voice and the disturbed feelings that nevertheless come through that voice. Although Nick never overtly expresses strong emotions, something is eating away at him as the silkworms eat away at the mulberry leaves. Because the story invites us to sympathize with Nick, to enter into his consciousness and view many things as he does, we also find his disturbed feelings to be disturbing. The gathering force of these disturbed and disturbing feelings underneath Nick's overt gentle voice transforms "Now I Lay Me" from a zephyr to a tornado.

The story is ethically disconcerting because in pulling us to sympathize with Nick, to share the feelings associated with his condition, it asks us to assent to some questionable values, especially those underlying the story's analogy between war and marriage, and, more particularly, between mortar shells and women.[3] And with this point, we can see how much the cognitive, the emotive, and the ethical are interlocking components of our experience. The better we comprehend the story's structure and techniques the more we can clarify – and deepen – the emotional engagement it offers. The deeper our emotional engagement the more we are implicated in the value structure on which Hemingway builds the story. Since the cognitive, emotive, and the ethical components of reading are so interdependent, problems within any one are likely to ripple through the others. With "Now I Lay Me," I eventually focus on the troublesome relationships between the ethical and emotive components of our experience. Before I get to those relationships, however, I want to develop a fuller account of how the whole story engages us cognitively and emotionally as we move from beginning to end. Finally, after this examination of "Now I Lay Me," I briefly sketch its similarities to and differences from a few other stories in *Men without Women*.

The Narrative Situation

As with any first-person narration, it is helpful to examine the narrative situation: who is telling the story to whom under what conditions (time, place, and other details of setting). Unlike, say, *Heart of Darkness*, which carefully specifies Marlow and his audience in time and place, or even *The Great Gatsby*, which situates Nick Carraway in the Midwest shortly after his eventful year on the East Coast, "Now I Lay Me" contains very little evidence about its occasion of narration. Like Jake Barnes of *The Sun Also Rises* and Frederic Henry of *A Farewell to Arms,* Nick Adams is telling his tale to an unspecified audience on an unspecified occasion. We know that some time has passed between the summer of sleepless nights and the time of the telling, but we don't know exactly how much.[4] This lack of specification has consequences for our understanding. Because Nick's audience is uncharacterized and the occasion undefined, we are more likely to feel directly addressed by him. Furthermore, the lack of specification invites us to fill in some details of the telling situation, especially as we try to supply an answer to the question of why Nick is telling this story, why Hemingway chooses to make Nick's monologue a metamemory. The title provides an important clue in its use of the present tense and its invocation of the well-known child's bedtime prayer:

> Now I lay me down to sleep
> I pray the Lord my soul to keep.
> If I should die before I wake
> I pray the Lord my soul to take.

Nick the teller is in much the same psychological state as Nick the soldier. Although he may no longer worry that his soul will go out of his body if he falls asleep, Nick is still living with deep wounds that disturb his nights. Just as his memories during that summer were efforts to cope with his war trauma, his memories of those memories are efforts to cope with his current condition.

The unspecified distance in time between that summer and the time of narration and the tense shifts throughout the monologue indicate the continuing power of Nick's memories, their significance for his current sense of self. On this account, Nick's telling is itself the main action in "Now I Lay Me," and Nick the teller is the ultimate focus of the story; the twists and turns of his monologue are important less for what they tell about his past than for what they reveal about his current psychological and emotional condition.[5]

This claim has two important consequences for our understanding: First, although the text of "Now I Lay Me" consists only of Nick's monologue, the story is more than that. Although Nick's monologue is devoted primarily to his past, Hemingway's larger story is about Nick in the present time of the telling. To understand the story we must read Nick's present state through what he says about his past and how he says it. Second, the story is essentially lyric in structure. The main action takes place inside Nick's consciousness and focuses not on any change in that consciousness but rather on revealing and exploring its contours and the broader context of its existence. In reading the story, we are invited to participate not only in coming to understand that consciousness but also in the feelings associated with it. In other words, the emotive force of "Now I Lay Me" depends largely on our sharing Nick's feelings in the way that we share the feelings of the speaker of a lyric poem such as Frost's "Stopping by Woods on a Snowy Evening" or Wordsworth's "I Wandered Lonely as a Cloud." The ethical force of the story depends on the way in which this participation implicates us in a set of values that tacitly underlie the whole story.

Nick's Strange Beginning

Nick's first paragraph is a very peculiar introduction, one that begins in one direction and then quickly veers off in another:

That night we lay on the floor in the room and I listened to the silkworms eating. The silk-worms fed in racks of mulberry leaves and all night you could hear them eating and a dropping sound in the leaves. I myself did not want to sleep because I had been living for a long time with the knowledge that if I ever shut my eyes in the dark and let myself go, my soul would go out of my body. I had been that way for a long time, ever since I had been blown up at night and felt it go out of me and go off and then come back. I tried never to think about it, but it had started to go since, in the nights, just at the moment of going off to sleep, and I could only stop it by a very great effort. So while now I am fairly sure that it would not really have gone out, yet then, that summer, I was unwilling to make the experiment. (*Complete Stories* 276)

The first three words ("That night we") indicate that the speaker is about to narrate his memory of an event. Yet in the rest of the first sentence, something curious happens to the narrative movement: *"we* lay on the floor" but only *"I"* listened to the silk-worms. Although Nick has a story to tell about "we," he no sooner begins it than he shifts his focus to "I." The shift becomes more surprising when we learn in the second half of the story that John, the other half of the "we," asks Nick, "You hear those damn silk-worms?" (*Complete Stories* 280). Why would Nick the teller shift from "we" to "I" when he knows that "we" listened? More generally, what can we infer about Nick based on this sudden shift from "we" to "I" and on the long delay before he returns to "that night"? Part of the answer is suggested by what we have already seen about the narrative situation. Despite his retrospective stance, Nick has not fully formulated the story he is about to tell; indeed, he is less focused on the narrative than on the feelings that motivate his memories. Furthermore, the sudden veering away suggests that, although he is drawn to recall "that night" there may be something unpleasant in the memory. The movement of the first sentence suggests that Nick has an approach/avoidance conflict with the specific memory of that night.

Initially, however, Nick's delay appears likely to be momentary as he moves to tell his audience why he "did not want to sleep" (*Complete Stories* 276). He does not have insomnia but fear. He can easily fall asleep but believes that if he does, his soul will go out of his body as he felt it go when he was wounded.[6] Nick gives only a clipped, truncated account of that experience: "I had been blown up at night and felt [my soul] go out of me and go off and then come back" (*Complete Stories* 276). For all its matter-of-factness, the description is sufficiently disturbing to render Nick's fear perfectly understandable. Nick the soldier has recovered from his physical wounding but not its psychic effects. Yet, the last sentence of the paragraph indicates that Nick the teller has developed sufficient distance from the physical event to overcome his fear of falling asleep in the dark. He can talk about the experience and his fear with considerable equanimity: "So while *now* I *am* fairly sure that it would not really have gone out, yet *then, that summer* I *was* unwilling to make the experiment" (*Complete Stories* 276, emphasis mine).

The movement of Nick's telling in the first paragraph thus

suggests that Nick has gotten further in coming to terms with his physical wounding than he has with his memories of "that night." But the paragraph also sets up strong associations between Nick's physical injury ("I had been blown up at night"), its spiritual and psychological consequences ("I tried never to think about it, but it [my soul] had started to go since, in the nights"), the memories of how he had spent "that night" and others, and his situation "now" as he recalls those nights. This chain suggests that whatever Nick uncovers about any of its links will have consequences for the others. Both this chain and Nick's matter-of-fact telling constitute a strong invitation to empathize with him – to see the world through his eyes and to share the feelings accompanying such a vision.

Apparently not yet ready to return to what happened "that night," Nick offers his recollections of two different kinds of memories: of fishing and of his parents. During the fishing memories, the distinctions between Nick as older teller and Nick as younger soldier begin to blur. The focus of the monologue shifts from what "sometimes" happened during those summer nights to what "sometimes" happened while fishing, until the two kinds of happenings are no longer distinct. Thus, Nick speaks in the present tense about the lasting effect of his memories: "Some of those streams I still remember and think that I have fished in them, and they are confused with streams I really know" (*Complete Stories* 277).

In merging Nick the teller and Nick the soldier, Hemingway develops further the analogy implicit in the narrative situation: the correspondence between Nick's telling now and his remembering then. Nick the soldier's memories are a way to handle his fear of sleep, a way to keep his soul connected to his body; his memories of fishing are a way to reconstruct his identity through both the care involved in the detailed memory and the reminder of the discipline of the sport. And as we see most dramatically in "Big Two-Hearted River," fishing has been a source of healing for Nick. Nick the teller's memories of those memories are designed to reconnect him with a disciplined, healing self. Apparently, he needs such a reconnection before returning to what happened the night he listened to the silkworms.

Nick's telling at this point is overtly lyric. He is not describing a sequence of events that occurred on any one fishing trip but rather evoking the mood and sensibility of many trips. Within that lyric presentation, we see Nick not only as devoted and disciplined but also as sensitive to other creatures: Salamanders are too "neat and agile and . . . lovely" in color to be used for bait, and he will not use crickets "because of the way they acted about the hook" (*Complete Stories* 277). It is relatively easy here to participate in Nick's feelings.

In the next movement of the monologue, Nick remembers the nights when he "could not fish" (*Complete Stories* 277), and so turned to praying for "all the people [he] had ever known" (*Complete Stories* 277). As a soldier Nick turned from (remembering) fishing to (remembering) people, presumably when his fear became too great for the fishing memories to occupy his mind sufficiently. The turn to people is a turn to more compelling – and potentially more disturbing – subjects. Nick the teller seems at some level to recognize this potential because he initially keeps himself at a greater distance from Nick the soldier than he did during the fishing memories. He preserves that distance by switching from first person to second and from assertions ("I could not fish") to conditionals ("If you try . . . you remembered") (*Complete Stories* 277). Nevertheless, in the middle of this distanced perspective, in the space between the dashes of the longest sentence in the story, Nick the teller again merges with Nick the soldier:

That took up a great amount of time, for if you try to remember all the people you have ever known, going back to the earliest thing you remember – which was, with me, the attic of the house where I was born and my mother and father's wedding cake in a tin box hanging from one of the rafters, and, in the attic, jars of snakes and other specimens that my father had collected as a boy and preserved in alcohol, the alcohol sunken in the jars so the backs of some of the snakes and specimens were exposed and turned white – if you thought back that far, you remembered a great many people. (*Complete Stories* 277)

The return to the first person ("with me") signals the merging as does the detailed dwelling on the contents of the memory: In describing what he remembered then, Nick is also remembering

54

now. Richard Hovey and other psychoanalytic critics make much of the images of cake and snakes, and their links to male and female genitalia, which in turn link the whitened snakes in alcohol to fears of castration. I acknowledge this psychoanalytic dimension of the passage, but I want to call attention to other, less often noticed elements. First, there is the switch from *"people you have ever known"* to "the earliest *thing* you remember." The things stand for the people: the cake for Nick's mother and father together – ominously hanging from the rafters as if the marriage it symbolizes has become suicidal – and the snakes for Nick's father alone. Why does Nick substitute these things for his parents, and why does he isolate his father in memory here?

The second striking feature of the sentence, especially in comparison to the fishing memories, is that Nick the teller quickly separates from his merging with Nick the soldier. After the dash, Nick returns to the conditional form and the second person and maintains that posture for the rest of the paragraph. He also shifts away from the memory of people and things to the memory of praying for people, though the prayers, "Hail Mary" and "Our Father," are easily associated with images of Nick's parents.[7] The psychological dynamics of these shifts are similar to those operating in the story's opening sentence: Nick the teller approaches the act of remembering his parents, especially his father, and then swerves away. Again, the situation seems to be one of approach/avoidance.

After focusing successively on people, things, and prayer, Nick turns to events; he also drops the second person and the conditional: "I tried to remember everything that had ever happened to me. . . . I found I could only remember back to that attic in my grandfather's house. Then I would start there and remember this way again, until I reached the war" (*Complete Stories* 277). It is as if Nick, having turned away from a painful memory, is readying himself for another attempt at facing it.

Narratives within the Monologue

In the two narratives of burning, Nick boldly forges ahead. Hemingway marks the new movement of the progression with a shift to the present tense – "I remember" – and a return to the narrative mode. With the shift to the present, Hemingway shows Nick bypassing the step of remembering himself remembering, leaping over that summer of memories and directly recalling events of his boyhood. At the same time, Hemingway ends the first, short narrative by linking this present time memory with memories Nick the soldier had: After twice repeating the phrase "I remember," Hemingway shifts back to the past, "I *could not remember* who burned the things even, and I would go on until I came to people and then stop and pray for them" (*Complete Stories* 278, emphasis mine). Hemingway treats the temporal perspective in much the same way in Nick's account of the second burning. He begins with "About the new house I remember" and then follows with the long account of what happened "one time" when his father returned from a hunting trip. Nick closes the account by returning to the past, "I would pray for them both" (*Complete Stories* 278).

The return to the narrative mode reinforces the sense that Nick is now articulating his most troubling memories. The detailed recounting in the second mini-narrative also marks it as the key moment in this first half of the story. As many readers have remarked, Nick finds the memory very painful because it shows his mother's smooth and effective power play over his father. She burns his father's possessions under the guise of "cleaning out the basement, dear" (*Complete Stories* 278) and his father is incapable of doing anything about it. Despite the pain of the memory, Nick's voice retains its tone of calm acceptance: "I stayed outside on the grass with the two game-bags. After a while I took them in" (*Complete Stories* 278). But in coming back to the summary sentence, Nick inadvertently reveals how the memory still wounds him, as Hemingway reconnects the memory of Nick the teller with that of Nick the soldier: "In remembering that, there were only two people, so I would pray for them both" (*Complete Stories* 278). The emotive force here is very powerful. We sense Nick's pain, both as witnessing child and as remembering adult, precisely because he tries to crase himself from the scene – despite what he says, we know that there were *three* people involved – even as we find the effort to focus on his parents and to keep his voice gentle deeply poignant.

Given what Nick has witnessed, we can easily understand why he first substituted things for his parents and why he isolates his father. Given what Nick has witnessed, we can also understand why in saying his prayers on "some nights . . . I could only get as far as 'On earth as it is in heaven' and then have to start all over and be absolutely unable to get past that" (*Complete Stories* 278). In the "Our Father" the line just before "On earth as it is in heaven" is "Thy will be done." Nick's father has been too weak to assert his will, and in his home it is "our mother" whose will is done. It's not that Nick forgets what comes next ("Give us this day our daily bread") but that he cannot envision his father as the true provider. And given what he has seen happen to his father, we can recognize how much his own anxiety about being a husband, a father, a provider is still plaguing Nick the teller.

Hemingway's handling of Nick's remarks about the "Our Father" is an instructive example of his art of omission, one that has implications for our interpretive decision about Nick's role in the burnings. Hemingway leaves out everything about the prayer except the one phrase "On earth as it is in heaven." He even has Nick say that "I could not remember my prayers" (*Complete Stories* 278). Once we supply the lines before and after "on earth as it is in heaven," we can readily infer the rest of Nick's psychological situation and overturn his own claim about not remembering. Because Hemingway's technique requires our active involvement in coming to understand Nick's situation, we become more deeply involved with Nick on the emotive level as well.

With regard to the narrative of the second burning, Nina Fournier cites biographical and manuscript evidence to suggest that Hemingway is again employing his art of omission. She sees Nick's reference to "only two people" as an act of denial and appeals to the evidence of the manuscripts where Hemingway has Mrs. Adams say that "Ernie," and then upon correction, "Nick," helped her with the burning. We therefore need to infer from the "thing left out" that much of the pain in Nick's memory – and the reason it is so difficult for him to return to it –

is that he was complicit in his mother's emasculation of his father.

This reading adds yet another layer to Nick's already complicated psychological dynamics, but suggest that here the thing left out actually falls away from the story. Hemingway deleted Mrs. Adams's line about Nick helping not because he wanted us to infer Nick's complicity but because he wanted to keep Nick in the observer role, to make him not an actor but a bystander. Although it is impossible to prove a negative (that Hemingway doesn't want readers to see Nick as having helped), I find it telling that Hemingway does not leave us a clue analogous to the one offered in "I could only get as far as 'On earth as it is in heaven.'" One likely place for Hemingway to have provided the clue is where Nick describes his mother's penchant for cleaning. By employing a somewhat ambiguous description such as "my mother was always having us clean things out. . . . At the end of one of these cleanings my father returned," Hemingway could have subtly signaled Nick's involvement. But Hemingway has Nick assign explicit and exclusive agency to his mother: "my mother was always cleaning things out. . . . One time . . . she made a good thorough cleaning out in the basement and burned everything" (*Complete Stories* 278).

I also favor the view that Nick is a witness rather than a participant in the scene between his parents because that role fits the logic of analogy on which the story is built. Just as the mortar shell hits Nick unawares, so too, does his mother's emasculation of his father. With this point, we can move beyond the particulars of the scene to the larger patterns of the story.

In traditional narrative, the logic of story is the logic of connected events: One thing happens which leads to another thing and so on until the author finds some way to resolve the sequence. In lyric narrative, the logic of event gives way to the logic of revelation and exploration of a character's emotions and attitudes in a particular situation. The movement from beginning to end typically follows the movement of the speaker's thoughts, but these thoughts are not typically a review of his or her identity and situation. Instead, as the speaker's thoughts follow their apparently autonomous direction, the author finds a way to convey a rounded awareness of the speaker's identity and situation. In "Now I Lay Me," Hemingway's strategy of revelation depends on a set of analogies. Nick the teller is analogous to Nick the soldier. Nick's physical wound is analogous to his psychic wound. Nick's parents, especially his mother who is the main actor in the psychic wounding, are analogous to the mortar shell that blew him up at night.

Given this analogical design, Nick's present-tense memory of the burnings provides the answer to the lingering question stemming from the first analogy: Why is Nick the teller in much the same condition as Nick the soldier? As we see from the end of the first paragraph, Nick is no longer afraid of falling asleep in the dark. What troubles him are the continuing effects of his psychic wounds, effects that make marriage and its concomitant intimacy with another human being impossible. If Nick the soldier needs some way of coping with the fear engendered by his having been blown up at night, Nick the teller needs some way of coping with the aftermath of that experience as it reminds him of an earlier analogous experience, one that he finds himself repeatedly recalling when he has difficulty going to sleep. The war wound is so psychically damaging because it is the second catastrophic experience of which Nick has been the victim. Even as this logic increases our sympathy for Nick, it complicates the ethical component of our reading. I shall return to this point after tracing the movement of the second half of Nick's monologue.

The Narrative of "That Night"

Having faced the most painful memory, Nick can then return to "that night" and the "silk-worms" of the story's first sentence. Although his physical wound is analogous to his psychic wound, there is a significant difference. Nick is not drawn to replay the scene of the bombing (note again how brief his description of the bombing is and that he stops his memories once he "reached the war" [277]). He is, however, drawn to think again and again about marriage. And now the approach/avoidance conflict becomes understandable. Nick's memories are painful enough to be capable of wounding him again, so naturally he wants to avoid them. Yet his desire for the intimacy he seems unable to have motivates him to keep returning to both the scene between his parents and the night he spent talking and thinking about marriage with John, a night clearly linked for him with his physical wounding. Furthermore, Hemingway's repeated references to the silkworms also become intelligible. He is establishing another analogy, between the instinctive and persistent eating of the silkworms and the instinctive and persistent replay of memory in Nick the soldier and Nick the teller. That the outcome of the silkworms' persistent activity is positive gives us some hope for the outcome of Nick's instinctive remembering.

The opening sequence of the conversation between Nick and John shows a surprising swing in Nick's attitudes. He is the one who asks John, "Do you want to talk a while?" (*Complete Stories* 279), but then only a few lines later he is the one who implies that they should stop talking: "Don't you think we'll wake them up, talking?" (*Complete Stories* 279). The sequence between these lines is worth a closer look.

> "Tell me about how you got married."
> "I told you that."
> "Was the letter you got Monday – from her?"
> "Sure. She writes me all the time. She's making good money with the place."
> "You'll have a nice place when you go back."
> "Sure. She runs it fine. She's making a lot of money."
> "Don't you think we'll wake them up, talking?" I asked. (*Complete Stories* 279)

Nick's ambivalence about marriage comes through in the double messages he sends here: He asks – indeed, commands – John to talk about marriage, but when John's talk is so positive ("she writes me all the time"; "she's making a lot of money") he suggests that they stop talking. Nick the soldier's ambivalent feelings are still shared by Nick the teller. He is returning to his memory of this night as a way to revisit those feelings, but as we see, revisiting them doesn't lead him to work through to any new attitudes.

After failing to heed Nick's gentle suggestion that they stop talking, John takes the lead in the conversation, commenting on the other men and his difference from them (they "sleep like pigs" but he is "nervous"), making small talk about smoking and the silkworms, and then asking Nick "is there something really the matter that you can't sleep?" Again the ensuing sequence is worth a close look:

> "I don't know, John. I got in pretty bad shape along early last spring and at night it bothers me."
> "Just like I am," he said. "I shouldn't have gotten in this war. I'm too nervous."
> "Maybe it will get better." (*Complete Stories* 280)

John's question offers Nick the opportunity to open up, to risk an intimate communication. Nick certainly does not embrace John's invitation ("I don't know") but he does not absolutely refuse it, since his rather general report ("I got in pretty bad shape along early last spring") leaves the door open for further questions about what exactly happened last spring. But John is too self-absorbed to go through that door and so he quickly assumes that he and Nick are two of a kind ("Just like I am"). Nick lets the door close by trying to reassure John rather than trying to explain that it's not nervousness that keeps him awake at night.[8]

A little later, the pattern repeats and then the conversation returns to marriage. Nick asks John, "How are your kids?" John replies that "they're fine," that they're the reason he can be an orderly rather than on the front line and that "They're fine kids but I want a boy. Three girls and no boy. That's a hell of a note." Nick, who will probably never have a family, can't take any more. Once again he tries to end the conversation: "Why don't you try and go to sleep?" (*Complete Stories* 280–1). John, slow on the uptake, again misses the hint and instead turns the conversation back to Nick's inability to sleep:

> "No, I can't sleep now. I'm wide awake now, Signor Tenente. Say, I'm worried about you not sleeping though."
> "It'll be all right, John. . . ."
> "You got to get all right. A man can't get along that don't sleep. Do you worry about anything? You got anything on your mind?"

"No, John, I don't think so."

"You ought to get married, Signor Tenente. Then you wouldn't worry."

"I don't know."

"You ought to get married. Why don't you pick out some nice Italian girl with plenty of money? You could get any one you want. You're young and you got good decorations and you look nice. You been wounded a couple of times."

"I can't talk the language well enough."

"You talk it fine. To hell with talking the language. You don't have to talk to them. Marry them." (*Complete Stories* 281)

There are two important differences in this repetition of the earlier pattern: Nick does not give John any opportunity to find out more about what is really wrong with him, and John's self-absorption shows not in his direct identification with Nick but in his confident recommendation of marriage as the cure for Nick's ailments. John's idea of marriage clearly does not include either equality or emotional intimacy; instead, it emphasizes material comfort ("marry the one with the most money," he says a few lines later) and sexual release (I don't suppose I'm the only one who hears other verbs underneath "marry" in John's recommendation, "Marry them.") After John articulates this view of marriage, Nick more forcefully moves to end the conversation, twice saying "let's sleep a while," and finally succeeds.

Why should Nick be remembering this conversation? In his current psychically wounded state, Nick is drawn back to it because it is both reassuring and alluring. Nick envies John's satisfaction with his own family life, even as he feels superior to the view of marriage that John advocates. The act of remembering functions for Nick as a (false) reassurance that he is right not to get married (if marriage is as John describes it), even as it shows us how much he desires a better marriage than the one his parents had or one following John's model.

Having replayed the conversation, Nick is now ready to conclude his metamemory. He recalls that though John did go right back to sleep (no surprise there), he "had a new thing to think about": "all the girls I had ever known and what kind of wives they would make" (*Complete Stories* 281). Nick the soldier tried to imagine taking John's advice. In a short time, however, Nick lost interest and went back to thinking about trout fishing because "the girls, after I had thought about them a few times, blurred and I could not call them into my mind and finally they all blurred and all became rather the same and I gave up thinking about them almost altogether" (*Complete Stories* 282). In a sense, he too successfully adopts John's view: He cannot retain his memories of individual women. Consequently, with this recollection, unlike his earlier ones, Nick the teller does not merge with Nick the soldier, does not recall any of the women he might have married. In the present, the possibility of marriage is not real enough for him to consider it. Consequently, Nick the teller suddenly leaves the events of that particular night and comments on the last time he saw John.

But I kept on with my prayers and I prayed very often for John in the nights and his class was removed from active service before the October offensive. I was glad he was not there, because he would have been a great worry to me. He came to the hospital in Milan to see me several months after and was very disappointed that I had not married and *I know he would feel very badly if he knew that, so far, I have never married.* He was going back to America and he was very certain about marriage and knew it would fix up everything. (*Complete Stories* 282, emphasis mine)

The passage completes the monologue not only because it recounts the aftermath of "that night" but also because the penultimate sentence brings Nick and his audience into the present of the telling and states the main fact of Nick's existence. In addition, the passage calls attention one last time to the difference between John's and Nick's views of marriage. John is confident that the kind of marriage he recommends would fix everything for Nick, but Nick obviously lacks that confidence. Nick, of course, is right: John's view of marriage is too narrow, and, indeed, too sexist to provide the kind of intimacy Nick wants – and could most benefit from. Ironically, Nick's psychic wounds are such that they keep him from what he most needs to heal. The analogical structure of the story indicates that, for Nick the teller, getting married would be much like falling asleep in the dark for Nick the soldier. Both events would leave him vulnerable to the sensation of getting "blown up at night," of having his soul leave his body. For some one who has experienced that twice already, putting himself in a situation where it could happen a third time is just too hard – even if he is deeply desirous of that situation. How much easier to think about fishing – even if those thoughts eventually lead him back to the topic of marriage.

Just as Nick the soldier's memories got him through the night but did not overcome his fear, so too Nick the teller's memories pass the time without enabling him to resolve anything. In this respect, the persistent activities of the silkworms are clearly more productive than Nick's persistent memories. As it reaches its conclusion, "Now I Lay Me" completes its revelation of what it's like to be in Nick's situation, and positions us to participate in the feelings associated with that situation. Nick's voice of gentle resignation actually enhances our sense of how deeply he is wounded; precisely because it cannot mask all his pain. Unlike John, we have access to what ails Nick – both in the past and in the present – and unlike John, we can see no easy cures. It is these elements that make "Now I Lay Me" a zephyr with the force of a tornado.

Emotion and Ethics

To be emotionally engaged with Nick's condition is also to assent, at least provisionally, to the story's value structure. Before I take up the troublesome element of that structure we have already identified – the analogy between mortar shells and wives – let us reflect on its other main elements: kindness, discipline, courage, and intimacy. As I reflect on the ethical components of the story, my own value structure necessarily comes into play, and I must therefore qualify the claims I make in this section. Because one of my own beliefs is that there are multiple admirable value systems, I offer the conclusions of this section not in a spirit of superiority to either Hemingway or other readers but in a spirit that seeks give-and-take about how the story depends on an implicit value structure and how flesh and blood (as opposed to authorial) readers might respond to that structure.

That kindness and sensitivity are implicitly part of the story's value structure is everywhere apparent: in Nick's attitudes as fisherman, in his prayers for others, especially his mother and father, and in his solicitousness toward John. To share in Nick's feelings is, in part, to share his fellow feeling and in that sense the ethical consequences are very positive ones.

To participate in the story also entails admiring Nick's careful discipline as a fisherman and as the orchestrator of memories during his summer of sleepless nights. Here the situation is more complicated. First, it is important to remember that Nick's monologue is not itself a model of disciplined reconstruction, a fact that qualifies the story's commitment to this value. Second, we need to ask whether the discipline of Nick the soldier functions positively or negatively, whether, that is, it enables him to get through the nights as well as can be expected or whether it is a means for him to repress feelings that he needs to face. The answer here seems to be both: Nick is, as we have noted, in fearful flight from the experience of his physical wounding, at the same time, his routines take him back to the scene of his first painful psychic wounding, and although he does not resolve anything through his memories, he is able to look clearly at the source of that wound. Furthermore, the discipline is connected with the kindness and sensitivity: Having exposed himself to the wound, Nick is nevertheless able to pray for the "two people" in the scene.

The value of discipline is also linked to the most famous of Hemingway's values, courage – also frequently called grace under pressure. What's important about the value in "Now I Lay Me" is not that Nick displays any great courage in any of the events he tells about; he is after all a victim in the two scenes of wounding he reports. The courage here is found in what I have identified as the main action of the story: Nick's act of telling. It is found in the gentle resignation of his voice, his ability to report his painful memories in such a straightforward manner. Nick's telling reveals him to be a man well aware of his feelings, even if he does not understand them all; the telling also reveals him to be a narrator who respects both the intelligence and the sensitivity of his audience.

This last point takes us to the story's evaluation of intimacy.

We find that value not just in what's implied by Nick's rejection of John's view of marriage, and not just in our larger sense that Nick both needs and is afraid of intimacy. We find it above all in the main action of the story: Nick's telling offers an intimate sharing that he never achieves with John and that he seems afraid of trying to achieve with a woman. Again the narrative situation makes a difference in our ethical experience. Because Nick's audience is never characterized, we are more likely to feel ourselves the direct recipients of his intimate sharing. But we also remain aware of Hemingway as the secret sharer, the one who designs Nick's monologue and trusts us to see more in it than Nick himself realizes. Lyric narrative is built on the value of intimacy.

The story's analogy between the mortar shell and Nick's mother pulls in the opposite direction from the rest of its ethical underpinnings. If I am right that the analogy is a crucial building block, that we can't reach our cognitive understanding of Nick's situation without recognizing the analogy, then the pull is very strong indeed. To feel with Nick is also to assent to Hemingway's implicit assumptions that (some) women are castrating bitches and that their malevolent force is very much like that of a mortar shell exploding in a trench. Without the analogy, the logic of the story doesn't work. With the analogy, the ethical component of the story is seriously compromised.

Because the analogy is so fundamental to the structure of the story, both cognitively and ethically, I see no way of mitigating its effect other than claiming that we ought not view Nick's mother as having any larger representative or thematic function – or indeed, any role – in conveying Hemingway's attitude toward women while he is writing "Now I Lay Me." This claim is not very persuasive, however, precisely because fictional narrative typically depends on thematizing for its significance. If we cannot see Mrs. Adams as having any thematic function, then we cannot see Nick as having any. But the power of "Now I Lay Me" depends, in part, on the premise that Nick represents more than a single, fictional character.

Given the importance to the story of the analogy between women and mortar shells, my emotional engagement with

Nick – and my relation to Hemingway as secret sharer – becomes much more ambivalent. Because the lyric structure invites my participation in Nick's feelings and Hemingway's values, I am now uncomfortable about sharing the intimacy the story offers. I find that I can neither repudiate nor fully celebrate the experience it offers. Instead, I retain my admiration for Hemingway's brilliant handling of the story's technique and become caught between my respect for much of its ethical basis and my instinctive rejection of the fundamental analogy. Being entangled in this ambivalence is a major reason the story is so disconcerting.

"Now I Lay Me" and *Men without Women*

With its focus on marriage and loss, "Now I Lay Me" shares thematic concerns with several other stories in *Men Without Women,* notably "In Another Country," "A Canary for One," and "Hills Like White Elephants." Although the collection contains no other lyric narrative, each of these other marriage stories demonstrates a technical brilliance similar to that of "Now I Lay Me" – although none of them is built on a problematic ethical base. In "A Canary for One," Hemingway juxtaposes the story of an American woman who prohibits her daughter's marriage to a Swiss with the implied story of the failure of the marriage between the narrator and his wife. The technical brilliance of the story lies in the way Hemingway gradually leads up to the revelation of its last sentence, "We were returning to Paris to set up separate residences" (*Complete Stories* 261). This revelation, a kind of appropriate surprise, requires us to reinterpret much of the dialogue between the narrator's wife and the American mother: Both the latter's insistence that "Americans make the best husbands" (*Complete Stories* 260) and the former's account of the early days of her marriage acquire ironic overtones. Furthermore, the final revelation presents the narrator's attitudes toward the American "lady" and her story in a new way: she is not just uninformed but completely out of touch. The technique makes us feel the failure of the couple's marriage with great force, and these feelings are linked to the story's basic values of intimacy and love.

In "Hills Like White Elephants," Hemingway represents the loss of intimacy between Jig and her male companion once they face the question of how to deal with Jig's pregnancy. In Jig's view, she and her companion "could have everything" (*Complete Stories* 213), but their efforts to discuss their situation impel her to ask "please please please please please please please please stop talking" (*Complete Stories* 214). Hemingway demonstrates his mastery of technique here by using dialogue itself as action. The breakdown of the couple's communication in the scene at the train station signals a larger breakdown in their relationship. "Hills" makes a striking contrast with "Now I Lay Me" because it places the woman in the ethically superior position, but the ethical basis is not an inversion of the one in "Now I Lay Me." Jig's companion, despite his inability to hear her, genuinely wants things to work out between them.

In "In Another Country," Hemingway creates in the old major a man who has had the kind of marriage that Nick longs for. Characteristically, Hemingway emphasizes not the marriage itself but the major's reaction to his wife's death. His deep grief and his ability to overcome it and go on have similarities with Nick's situation in "Now I Lay Me." Hemingway's technical brilliance here lies in his simultaneous representation of the major's situation and its implied effect on the young narrator, a character much like, though never definitively identified as, Nick. The ethical basis of "In Another Country" is firmly rooted in love and courage, and despite its emphasis on loss, the heroic figure of the major gives it the most positive view of human possibility in all of *Men without Women*.

This brief look at other, thematically similar stories allows us to return to "Now I Lay Me" with both reassurance and disappointment. The ethical problems of the story are not everywhere in *Men without Women*, but the contrast highlights their presence even more. "Now I Lay Me" remains for me the most powerful and most disconcerting story in the collection. On a sleepless night, I can imagine slowly rereading – or just recalling – it from beginning to end. Like Nick's memories of his parents, the fascination of the story remains no matter how many times I go over it. Indeed, as I do my version of Nick's repetitive memories, I find myself slightly revising Hemingway's title: He might well have called it "Now I Lay Me Down to Read."

NOTES

1. The term was coined by Peter J. Rabinowitz; for further discussions see his "Truth in Fiction," and *Before Reading* as well as my *Narrative as Rhetoric*, especially the Introduction and Chapters 7 and 9.

2. Frequently, lyric and narrative are defined according to the difference between "sequence of events" and "static situation." I believe that this distinction captures tendencies of each genre rather than the essential identifying features of each. For a fuller account of the relation between lyric and narrative, see Chapter 1 of my *Narrative as Rhetoric*, "Judgment in Lyric and Narrative: Toward an Understanding of Audience Engagement in *The Waves*."

3. The story does not explicitly identify how Nick "had been blown up at night" (*Complete Stories* 276) but leaves us to supply the answer. He has been hit by some piece of artillery, and it is certainly plausible to infer that it was a mortar shell.

4. The story does let us know that Nick the soldier is in Italy during World War I because "they had taken [John] for a soldier in nineteen fourteen" and John calls Nick "Signor Tenente." The reference to the "October offensive," a bloody affair in which many Italians were killed and which John was fortunate to miss, (*Complete Stories* 282) allows us to place Nick the soldier in the summer of 1918. Although the date on which Nick the teller remembers that summer is unspecified, the last sentence of the first paragraph suggests that it is years rather than weeks or months later: "So while *now* I am fairly sure that [my soul] would not really have gone out [of my body], yet *then, that summer,* I was unwilling to make the experiment" (*Complete Stories* 276; emphasis mine).

5. Although the story has received some fine critical commentary, few critics have analyzed the narrative technique in detail and no one, to my knowledge, has given it the kind of scrutiny I attempt here. DeFalco, Hovey, and Brenner have offered illuminating psychoanalytic readings. Flora, in an extended discussion, situates it in relation to the other Nick Adams stories, and reminds us that the monologue is a memory. Steinke develops a nice comparison with "In Another Country"; Josephs relates the story to Hemingway's own out of body experience, and Scafella links it to Emersonian philosophy. Fournier

cites the evidence of the manuscripts to argue that Hovey's psycho-analytic interpretation overemphasizes the theme of castration; in Fournier's view, it is a marriage story, and she offers an insightful account of the progression of Nick's memories in the first half of the story. Scholes and Comley effectively show how the story fits with Hemingway's negative portrayal of mothers.

In addition to focusing some attention on matters of form, all these critics, to one extent or another, regard the main interpretive task as thematizing the story either in relation to other Nick Adams stories or to Hemingway's own life. Nick's memories of the burnings are typically read as based on Hemingway's memories of similar events in his own life, a tendency encouraged by study of the manuscripts at the John F. Kennedy Library. One of the manuscripts shows that at one point Hemingway had Mrs. Adams say "and Ernie's helped me burn the things" (Kennedy Library/EH 618). I discuss this evidence shortly, but my interest here is less in the biographical issues, intriguing as they are, and more in how the story invites its reader to participate in Nick's situation.

6. Allen Josephs argues that Nick is describing what medical experts now call an "out of body experience," in which a person's consciousness detaches completely from the physical body. Whether Nick's experience of wounding (or Hemingway's, for that matter) conforms to the clinical definition of an out of body event is arguable, but Josephs' essay nicely emphasizes that Nick is all too able to fall asleep.

7. For more on this point, see Fournier's impressive close reading. For those interested in the biographical connections, it is perhaps worth pointing out that Hemingway's mother's name was Grace, so just as Nick's "Hail, Mary, full of grace" recalls Mrs. Adams for him, it also recalls Grace Hall Hemingway for his creator.

8. In light of the recent critical interest in Hemingway's complex attitudes toward and representations of sexuality (see especially the work by Moddelmog and Scholes and Comley), I think it is important to note that the situation here – two men lying near each other at night unable to sleep – invites us to look for homoerotic overtones in the interaction between Nick and John but that the interaction itself indicates a lack of such overtones. One cannot prove a negative, but the conversation moves not toward but away from intimacy and Nick and John are both more preoccupied with their private worlds than they are concerned with connecting. Given this apparent lack

of interest in connecting during that night, I am not inclined to see Nick's memory of it as a replay of his homoerotic desire for John. In "A Simple Enquiry," by contrast, Hemingway uses the dialogue between the major and his orderly to explore the complications of same sex desire in a situation where it is combined with power differentials and a strong prohibition. Part of the power of "A Simple Enquiry" depends on its leaving open the question of the orderly's desire (he claims he is not "corrupt," but the story closes with the major wondering "if he lied to me" [251, 252]). The similar questions about Nick's and John's desire seem closed off in "Now I Lay Me."

WORKS CITED

Brenner, Gerry. *Concealments in Hemingway's Works.* Columbus: Ohio State University Press, 1983.

DeFalco, Joseph. *The Hero in Hemingway's Short Stories.* Pittsburgh: University of Pittsburgh Press, 1963.

Flora, Joseph. *Hemingway's Nick Adams.* Baton Rouge: Louisiana State University Press, 1982.

Fournier, Nina. *Father, Mother, and Son: A Study of the Manuscripts of Ernest Hemingway's "Indian Camp," "Now I Lay Me," and "Fathers and Sons".* Trinity College (CT): M.A. Thesis, 1991.

Hemingway, Ernest. *The Complete Short Stories of Ernest Hemingway.* New York: Charles Scribner's Sons, 1987.

Hovey, Richard B. "Hemingway's 'Now I Lay Me': A Psychological Interpretation." *Literature and Psychology* 15 (1965):70–8.

Josephs, Allen. "Hemingway's Out of Body Experience." *Hemingway Review* 2.2 (Spring 1983):11–17.

Moddelmog, Debra. "Reconstructing Hemingway's Identity: Sexual Politics, the Author, and the Multicultural Classroom." *Narrative* 1 (1993):187–206.

"Protecting the Hemingway Myth: Casting out Forbidden Desires from *The Garden of Eden. Prospects: An Annual Journal of American Cultural Studies* (1996):189–221.

Phelan, James. *Narrative as Rhetoric: Technique, Audiences, Ethics, Ideology.* Columbus: Ohio State University Press, 1996.

Rabinowitz, Peter J. *Before Reading: Narrative Conventions and the Politics of Interpretation.* Ithaca: Cornell University Press, 1987.

"Truth in Fiction: A Reexamination of Audiences." *Critical Inquiry* 4 (1977):121–41.

Scafella, Frank. "'I and the Abyss,' Emerson, Hemingway, and the Modern Vision of Death." *Hemingway Review* 4.2 (Spring 1985):2–6.

"Imagistic Landscape of a Psyche: Hemingway's Nick Adams." *Hemingway Review* 2.2 (Spring 1983):2–10.

Scholes, Robert and Nancy R. Comley. *Hemingway's Genders.* New Haven: Yale University Press, 1994.

Steinke, James. "Hemingway's 'In Another Country' and 'Now I Lay Me.'" *Hemingway Review* 5.1 (Fall 1985):32–9.

Left: Virgin stand of white pine. *Source:* State Archives of Michigan.

Below: Burned-over clear-cut. *Source:* State Archives of Michigan.

4

Second Growth: The Ecology of Loss in "Fathers and Sons"

SUSAN F. BEEGEL

O, my father, our happiest days are o'er and gone into lasting oblivion and never again shall we enjoy our forest home. The eagle's eye could not even discover where once thy wigwam and thy peaceful fires were hid.
– Andrew Blackbird, 19th century Ojibway historian [1]

"We might as well say good-bye to it."
– Ernest Hemingway, "The Last Good Country"

Prologue

This summer, on the morning of Ernest Hemingway's July birthday, I was stuck at a traffic light during morning rush hour in the author's hometown of Oak Park, Illinois. In the stopped cars around me, commuters seized the moment's pause afforded by a red light to adjust air conditioning, rummage for documents in briefcases, and punch the day's first call into cellular phones. For myself, it seemed a good time to check my watch and the computer printout of my itinerary once more, and worry about making my flight out of Chicago's O'Hare Airport – until the screech of brakes caused me to look up just as a whitetail deer flashed across the busy intersection, against the light and through moving traffic. Leaping adroitly through the snarl of metal hoods and rubber tires, the doe reached the other side in safety, and went mincing calmly down an asphalt sidewalk, pausing now and again to browse a well-fertilized square of lawn, or yank at the foliage of someone's hedge.

I am indebted to my husband, botanist and ecologist Wesley Newell Tiffney, Jr., for all manner of help with this essay.

Why did the deer cross the intersection? Doubtless, in her own mind, to breakfast on grass and ornamental shrubbery. An ecologist would answer that – like exploding suburban populations of whitetail deer everywhere east of the Mississippi – she had successfully adapted to a new environment following the obliteration by Chicago's urban sprawl of the prairie grasslands that had nourished generations of her forebears. And an ecocritic would answer that the deer crossed the intersection to comment on the ecological education of Ernest Hemingway – whose own forebears were nourished by these now asphalted grasslands – and on that education's impact on "Fathers and Sons," the final tale in *Winner Take Nothing,* and Hemingway's last published Nick Adams story.

A Reading

"Fathers and Sons" begins in an uncharacteristic setting for a Hemingway short story, Main Street, Middle America, Sunday afternoon, but that setting is characteristically oppressive. Driving through this small town, Nick is constantly stopped by traffic lights that flash on and off despite the "traffic-less Sunday." The shade trees lining Main Street are "heavy. . . . only too heavy." They "shut out the sun" and "dampen the houses for a stranger" (*Complete Stories* 369). The unnamed village is as cloying as Krebs's hometown in the Oklahoma of "Soldier's Home," and in order to put it behind him as rapidly as possible, Nick chooses to ignore a detour sign, seeing that "cars had obviously gone through" and believing that "it was some repair which had been completed" (369). The action is a metaphor for the psychic journey that follows, as Nick enters emotional terrain he has previously avoided, to try to "complete repairs," or finish his grief work for his father, who has committed suicide.

There is a feeling of relief as Nick moves out "past the last house and onto the highway that rose and fell straight away ahead" (369). Beyond the town, "all of this country was good to drive through and to see," but neither Nick Adams nor his creator is a Kerouac, a Steinbeck, a Least Heat Moon, an American poet of the open road. Highway, in Hemingway, is a wound on the land, destroyer of a way of life. Shortly before writing "Fathers and Sons," Hemingway mourned the destruction by highway of Nick Adams's Michigan in a passage later deleted from *Death in the Afternoon:*

> Michigan I loved very much when I lived in it, and when I was away from it, but as I grew up each time I returned to it it was changed. It was a country of forests, lakes and streams and small farms with hills and pastures, always with a background of woods. There was no place in upper Michigan where you could look across open land and not see the woods and you were never far away from open water. They cut down the forests, the streams lost their water, the lakes had their levels lowered and raised by the taking or not taking of water to float sewerage from Chicago down the drainage canal; they built concrete motor roads across all the country and around the lakes; the motorists caught all the fish out of the streams and, as the boys went to Flint or Detroit to work and prices made it impossible to make a living, they abandoned the farms.[2] (quoted in Beegel 52–3)

This same sense of loss is present in "Fathers and Sons," where Nick perceives highway as laceration, with "banks of red dirt sliced cleanly away," and "second-growth forest on both sides" recalling the old-growth timber slashed to make way for the automobile. And so his drive across America is tinged with mourning for the land and for an expulsion from Eden.

Yet the highway carries Nick into "good country," where farms have not yet been abandoned ("the cotton was picked and in the clearings there were patches of corn, some cut with streaks of red sorghum"), and "driving easily" now, he begins to hunt the country in his mind, "sizing up each clearing as to feed and cover and figuring where you would find a covey and which way they would fly" (369). He remembers an important rule for quail hunting taught him by his father:

> In shooting quail you must not get between them and their habitual cover, once the dogs have found them, or when they flush they will come pouring at you, some rising steep, some skimming by your ears, whirring into a size you have never seen them in the air as they pass. (369)

Again "Fathers and Sons" offers a potent metaphor for grief work, as "hunting this country for quail as his father had taught him, Nicholas Adams started thinking about his father" (369). The land flushes memories, and in this story where love and grief, anger and guilt are winged things, they come pouring at Nick, who is, like the startled quail hunter, unprepared to take them. The metaphor is also good for the structure of this story – a speeding flock of associations that never coalesces or allows a reader an easy shot at interpretation.

The first thing Nick always thinks about when remembering his father is "the eyes . . . they saw much farther and much quicker than the human eye sees and they were the great gift his father had" (369–70). The father's vision identifies him with the American wilderness, with the world of nature under siege in this story: "his father saw as a big-horn ram or as an eagle sees, literally" (370). In an early draft of the story, his keen eyesight, together with his "hooked, hawk nose," his raptor's passion for hunting and fishing, and perhaps his symbolic Americanness ("They've run up the flag," is his first sentence), prompt the father's Indian friends to name him Me-teh-ta-la (exact spelling unclear in manuscript), which Hemingway tells us "means Eagle Eye" (Kennedy Library/EH 382; see also Paul Smith, *A Reader's Guide* 308). The published version, too, makes it clear that the eagle is the father's spirit animal.

To the Ojibway,[3] each animal is emblematic of a special power or gift. The eagle symbolizes not just sharp eyesight, but vision, the ability to draw wisdom from the past and to see into the future (Johnston 53, 55). When the Ojibway pray to the eagle, they ask for "vision, strength, and courage" to confront the challenges of the unknown path ahead (Johnston 55). The eagle, then, is an ironic choice of spirit animal for a father who has committed suicide in a story about a son seeking guidance from memories of his father.

Like all faculties "that surpass human requirements," the father's eagle vision is a curse as well as a "great gift," close to a species of mental illness, making the father "very nervous" (370). The ability to see more means the necessity of feeling more; acute senses are easily lacerated. Eagle Eye is sentimental, susceptible to feeling, and "like most sentimental people . . . both cruel and abused. . . . All sentimental people are betrayed so many times" (370). As a result of his "gift," the father "die[s] in a trap he had helped only a little to set" (370), and the trap here, we are sure, is steel-jawed and not humane, as suicide is, psychologically, a death by slow torture.

Only a little later in the story, still thinking about his father's death, Nick reflects that "there were still too many people alive" for him to write it (371). Hemingway, always at his most auto-biographical in the Nick Adams stories, working in "Fathers and Sons" with material drawn from his own father's 1928 suicide, clearly shared Nick's problem. Manuscripts of this short story contain a number of passages deleted by Hemingway prior to publication, passages that would have humiliated and enraged his mother and siblings – all very much alive when "Fathers and Sons" first appeared in *Winner Take Nothing*.

Today, more than sixty years after the short story's publication, excised material explains the "trap" that has claimed Nick's father – marriage to a woman with whom "he had no more in common than a coyote has with a white french poodle" (Kennedy Library/EH 383). Nick further qualifies the metaphor to underscore the father's weakness in submitting to such a relationship: "For he was no wolf, my father" (Kennedy Library/EH 383). Nick, who spends time "out at the ranch," would know that coyotes, who scavenge near human habitation and prey on young and injured livestock, are so successfully adapted to civilization that their populations sometimes thrive despite vigorous hunting, poisoning, and trapping. He would also know that the wolf, a creature of true wilderness, was a vanishing species, all but gone from the country where he camped and hiked in boyhood – Michigan's Upper Peninsula (Lopez 13). Both the coyote metaphor and its wolf qualifier comment not only on the father's marital predicament, but on the feminization of American culture, and the "endangerment" of traditional masculinity.

Cute and hackneyed, the marriage of persecuted coyote to pampered purebred is an image that critic Leslie Fiedler might describe as stereotypically "turning Mother into a monster of piety, who despises the great clean outdoors of rod and gun" (331). Hemingway was wise to leave it out. But the deleted passages that follow paint a picture of the miserable marriage, its audience of bewildered children, the father's fatal emasculation, and the son's contempt and pity so strong that this material might be returned to "Fathers and Sons" with profit:

Whoever, in a marriage of that sort, wins the first encounter is in command and, having lost, to continue to appeal to reason, to write letters at night, hysterically logical letters explaining your position, to have it out again before the children – then the inevitable making up, loser received by victor with some magnanimity, everything that had been told the children cancelled, the home full of love, and Mother carried you, darling, over her heart all those months and her heart beat in your heart. Oh yes and what about his heart and where did it beat and who beats it now and what a hollow sound it makes. (Kennedy Library/EH 383; also quoted in Paul Smith, *A Reader's Guide* 308)

More powerful still, and very strange, is the next deleted passage, detailing the exposure of the father's sexual frustration to his unwitting son:

I've seen him when we used to row in the boat in the evening, trolling, the lake quiet, the sun down behind the hills, widening circles where the bass rose, ask me to take the oars because it was too uncomfortable. "It's the hot weather," he said, "and the exercise."

I would row, not knowing what it was about, watching him sitting in the stern the bulk of him, the blackness of him, he was very big and his hair and beard were black, his skin was dark and he had an indian nose and those wonderful eyes and I didn't know what it was that made him so uncomfortable. I had not started to be uncomfortable that way yet. (Kennedy Library/EH 383; also quoted in Paul Smith, *A Reader's Guide* 309)

Paul Smith has noted how this passage evokes the ending of "Indian Camp," where "In the early morning on the lake sitting in the stern of the boat with his father rowing, [Nick] felt quite sure that he would never die" (*A Reader's Guide* 309; *Complete Stories* 70). Yet the manuscript of "Fathers and Sons" does not so much evoke as invert the ending of "Indian Camp." It is sunset, not sunrise; darkness is gathering. Sexuality intrudes on an

Edenic scene – the quiet lake, the rising fish – when a grown man alone with his young son has an erection. The child is at the oars, the father in the stern. The father's presence is not comforting, but physically threatening – "the *bulk* of him, the *blackness* of him, he was *very big* and his hair and beard were *black,* his skin was *dark."* Even the father's "indian nose" and "wonderful eyes," however admired by Nick, can be construed as savage and predatory. And under the circumstances, the threat may be read as sexual. Although it's not clear whether the father's unwanted erection has an object, or why the son, "not knowing what it was about" should perceive him as so ogrelike at this moment, there's a suggestion, if not of an unwanted impulse to homosexual incest on the father's part, of some unspoken way in which Dr. Adams' sexual frustration in marriage makes him appear dangerous to the child.

In the manuscript of "Fathers and Sons," these disturbing memories flow into a passage that also appears in the published story: "His father had summed up the whole matter by stating that masturbation produced blindness, insanity, and death, while a man who went with prostitutes would contract hideous venereal diseases and that the thing to do was to keep your hands off of people" (371). Isolated in the published short story, this passage can seem a simply humorous jab at the father's oldfashioned attitudes toward human sexuality – but the manuscripts suggest a more complex reading. Without sanctioned release from sexual tension in marriage, he suffers from a proliferation of urges that cannot be relieved.

"Unsound on sex" Nick labels his father with striking understatement, and in the published story gives us two splendidly comic rather than tragic instances of this unsoundness (370). When young Nick reads that opera singer Enrico Caruso has been arrested for "mashing" and asks his father what "mashing" means, the response, "a heinous crime," causes Nick to imagine "the great tenor doing something strange, bizarre, and heinous with a potato masher to a beautiful lady who looked like the pictures of Anna Held on the inside of cigar boxes" and to resolve "with considerable horror, that when he was old enough he would try mashing at least once" (371).[4]

81

The other moment occurs when Nick, bitten by a squirrel he has wounded, calls the animal a "dirty little bugger" without knowing what the noun means, and his father explains that "A bugger is a man who has intercourse with animals" (371). Again, the boy's imagination is "stirred and horrified" and "he thought of various animals but none seemed attractive or practical" (371). Like Nick's vision of mashing, this is a very funny moment in a text that is more often wrenching, and a tribute to the range of emotions Hemingway can play upon in the brief span of a short story. Yet these jokes may serve a more serious purpose. Both represent moments when a boy's normal sexual curiosity, lacking either a healthy role model or honest instruction, is channeled toward fetishism. Both are telling replacements for the deleted moments when Nick is *truly* "stirred and horrified" by what he learns about human sexuality from his parents' quarreling, and from his father in the rowboat.

The father's half-definition of "bugger" is particularly strange in this context. In common usage the noun "bugger" refers to a sodomite, a practitioner of anal intercourse, and only includes intercourse with animals when used as a technical term in criminal law. Hemingway must have expected readers at least to pause over Dr. Adams' unusual definition of buggery, making animals the objects of homosexual desires and practices. The joke resonates oddly in a story where hunting, fishing, and the father-son comradeship they engender are "passion[s]" that "never slacken" (370).

Except for their reverberations in the jokes, the deleted passages remain in the published text of "Fathers and Sons" only in a general way: "Now, knowing how it all had been, even remembering the earliest times before things had gone badly was not good remembering" (371). Nick knows that he can "get rid of" these memories by writing, but because it is "still too early" and there are "still too many people," he is denied that therapy for his grief (371). He decides to think about something else, but like most people obsessing on an unresolved problem, arrives only at the still more horrifying image of his dead father's shattered face as repaired by the undertaker (371).

Here "Fathers and Sons" incorporates harsh self-criticism. By suppressing his most painful memories and substituting humor, Nick-Hemingway has "only made certain dashingly executed repairs of doubtful artistic merit" (371). The short story does not present the real father any more than the undertaker presents the real face; rather, we are given a father prepared for public viewing – "It was a good story but there were still too many people alive for him to write it" (371). The momentary identification of Nick with the "proud and smugly pleased" undertaker reflects not only shame for planning to exploit the father's suicide in a story, but also for failing to tell that story honestly (371).

Nick flinches away from painful images of his father in the casket and his own shame at planning to exploit those images in his writing, and turns instead to thinking about his "education" in human sexuality "in the hemlock woods behind the Indian camp" (371). Just as Nick in "Now I Lay Me" seeks to exorcise memories of his parents' wretched marriage by fishing remembered trout streams in his mind, so Nick in "Fathers and Sons" makes a conscious effort to "feel all of that trail" to the Indian camp "with bare feet" (372), using the powerful actuality of his artist's memory to return to what he hopes will be therapeutic terrain:

First there was the pine-needle loam through the hemlock woods behind the cottage where the fallen logs crumbled into wood dust and long splintered pieces of wood hung like javelins in the tree that had been struck by lightning. You crossed the creek on a log and if you stepped off there was the black muck of the swamp. You climbed a fence out of the woods and the trail was hard in the sun across the field with cropped grass and sheep sorrel and mullen growing and to the left the quaky bog of the creek bottom where the killdeer plover fed. (372)

There is, however, no comfort in such a return, for Nick's memories must perforce include the destruction and exploitation of both the hemlock woods and the Indian way of life, as this description of the story's second penetrating road-wound makes plain:

Then . . . you went into the woods on the wide clay and shale road, cool under the trees, and broadened for them to skid out the hemlock bark the Indians cut. The hemlock bark was cut in long rows of stacks, roofed over with more bark, like houses, and the peeled logs lay huge and yellow where the trees had been felled. They left the logs in the woods to rot, they did not even clear away or burn the tops. It was only the bark they wanted for the tannery at Boyne City; hauling it across the lake on the ice in winter, and each year there was less forest and more open, hot, shadeless, weed-grown slashing. (372)

The wasteful assault on the Michigan forests encapsulated in these few sentences is historically accurate. After the Civil War, the lumber and forest products industries entered a phase of vigorous expansion, engendered by the development of new forms of transport, felling, and mill technology, as well as the creation of corporate monopolies (Williams 194). Michigan and other Lake states – with their dense, rich, and various tree cover, their low and gently rolling terrain, and their readily available water transport via lakes and rivers – became the site of frenzied exploitation, peaking at 10,000 million board feet per annum in 1890, falling off gradually to a still staggering 4,000 million board feet in 1910 (Williams 197, 198).[5] This timbering rampage was conducted entirely without today's concern for "sustainable" yields, and the impact on the Michigan of Nick Adams' boyhood was devastating. By 1907, more than 10.7 million acres of the state had been clearcut (Williams 236).[6] Lewis C. Reimann, a contemporary of Hemingway's, describes it this way:

Where once tall pine had stood dark and vast there now stretched vast tracts of wasteland. The cut-over areas were littered with refuse from hasty, grabbing lumbering; fire burned off what was left of brush and stumps; the unprotected topsoil was washed away by erosion; a tangle of wild pin cherries and hazel brush grew up in the scorched ground to be again exposed to frequent and destructive attacks by fire. The area offered no fit habitation for man or beast. Here and there a former lumberjack or trusting immigrant bought a piece of high ground from the deserting lumber operators to eke out a precarious living from the bare soil, the few stands of cedar in the swamps, and the game which had escaped the whirlwind of lumbering and fire. (37)

Hemingway's father, born in 1871, and Hemingway himself, born in 1899, reaped this whirlwind. The destruction of old-growth forests near the family's Michigan summer home meant that their shared passion for wilderness, hunting, and fishing would become a continuing source of shared grief and mourning. Indians sent young Ernest and his sister home when the children's wide-eyed fascination with logging operations grew unsafe (Miller 26). Later, father and son helped fight a slash-kindled forest fire that threatened the family cottage, and both were doubtless sickened when, in 1926, the county dynamited a road through the forest heart of the Hemingway property to provide access for a tourist hotel (Miller 5, 68).[7] Clearcut forests in Michigan were not replanted until the 1920s, and that first crop was not ready for harvest as saw timber until five years after Hemingway's 1961 suicide (Sommers 111). Aldo Leopold has written that "one of the penalties of an ecological education is that one lives alone in a world of wounds" (197).

Those wounds are everywhere apparent in the Nick Adams stories – in the burned over terrain of "Big Two-Hearted River" (the result of historic slash fires near Seney, Michigan [Jobst 24]), in the abandoned mill town of Hortons Bay in "The End of Something," and in the clearcuts of Hemingway's final, posthumously published Nick Adams story, the aborted novel "The Last Good Country": "'I hate them [the clearcuts],' his sister said. 'And the damn weeds are like flowers in a tree cemetery if no one took care of it'" (516). "Fathers and Sons," and the reduction of its hemlock forest to "open, hot, shadeless, weed-grown slashing," are a vital part of this lineage.

The forestry practices sketched in the hemlock bark passage of "Fathers and Sons" also had a devastating effect on the Ojibway, whose traditional lifestyle included hunting, fishing, and basic agriculture. The trees falling by billions of board feet to an aggressive lumber industry were life itself to a forest people. The Indians used the forest in a sustainable way for fruit and nuts, bark, sap, dyes, medicine, and arrow wood, cutting only dead or dying trees for firewood. Ojibway songs of praise indicate that the Indians worshipped the ability of trees to heal themselves and to give sustenance to man (Johnston 32–3). Sir James George Frazer asserts in *The Golden Bough* that "The Ojebways [sic] very seldom cut down green or living trees, from the idea that it puts them to pain, and some of their medicine men profess to have heard the wailing of the trees under the axe" (130).

The destruction of the forests left the Ojibway acculturated and dependent for low-paying jobs on the very industry that had stolen their way of life. The lumber industry lobbied in Washington for legislation that would permit the Ojibway to sell their allotments of reservation land (Writers' Program 32). Impoverished, the Indians often sold their property, for less than the value of its standing trees, to timber barons who evaded taxes by never claiming title (Reimann 32). Agents for the Bureau of Indian Affairs grew wealthy by conniving at such sales (Reimann 32).

In the despair and squalor of "Indian Camp," in half-breed Dick Boulton's insistence that "the logs are stolen" in "The Doctor and the Doctor's Wife," in the alcoholism and promiscuity of "Ten Indians," in the silent discomfort of Indians in a train station full of lumbermen and their prostitutes in "The Light of the World," the Nick Adams stories reveal Hemingway's familiarity with the Ojibway tragedy embodied in the annihilation of Michigan's old-growth forests. An integral part of this cycle, "Fathers and Sons" shows the Ojibway degraded into complicity with one of the most wasteful practices of the lumber industry – clearcutting entire hemlock forests to supply bark for tanning harness leather. And even the Indians' tenuous ability to eke out a living as bark peelers is foredoomed. The rise of the automobile and the consequent collapse of the harness industry ended demand for hemlock bark long before Hemingway began work on this story in 1932 or 1933 (Cox et al. 166–7; Paul Smith, *A Reader's Guide* 307–8).

Nick's effort not to think about the ravaged face of his dead father thus trends uncontrollably into grief and mourning for the Michigan woods and their Ojibway inhabitants, as Nick's memories of his father are inextricably intertwined with his memories of the land. Again, Nick flinches, and again, he makes an effort to divert the flow of memory into a more pleasant channel:

But there was still much forest then, virgin forest where the trees grew high before there were any branches and you walked on the

86

brown, clean, springy-needled ground with no undergrowth and it was cool on the hottest days and they three lay against the trunk of a hemlock wider than two beds are long, with the breeze high in the tops and the cool light that came in patches, and Billy said:

"You want Trudy again?" (372)

The gendered imagery in this sentence, with its virgin forest and willing Indian girl, is classically American, classically Edenic, and classically exploitative. As Annette Kolodny explains in *The Lay of the Land*, the Indian woman in white, Euro-American literature becomes "a kind of emblem for a land that was . . . entertaining the Europeans 'with all love and kindness . . . and as much bounty'" (5). Nick Adams' sexual enjoyment of Trudy partakes of the same "excitement that greeted John Rolfe's marriage to Pocahontas, in April of 1614 . . . serv[ing] in some symbolic sense, as a kind of objective correlative for the possibility of Europeans' actually possessing the charms inherent in the virgin continent" (Kolodny 5).

Nick Adams' Eden is more problematic. In "Fathers and Sons" both the virgin forest and its vast bedstead hemlock have been raped and exploited *before* they are visited in retrospect. That Trudy's fate will be no different from the fate of the generous land she embodies, the short story soon makes clear. Indeed, there is trouble in Eden before Nick's first sentence of remembrance is complete – there are three people, not two, in the hemlock paradise. The passage that follows elaborates on this problem. Billy Gilby's willingness to share his sister's sexual favors with his white friend Nick ("You want Trudy again?" [372]), and Trudy's utter unconsciousness of the "sins" of incest and voyeurism ("I no mind Billy. He my brother." [372]) suggest a truly prelapsarian innocence. The Indian children (if Nick is fifteen, then Trudy is twelve and Billy as young as nine if we read biographically) of "Fathers and Sons" regard sexuality as completely natural, unfettered by any culturally imposed notions of wrongdoing.[8]

Critics have noted the comic aspects of Nick's dalliance with Trudy while Billy looks on (Flora 240; Paul Smith, *A Reader's Guide* 314), and lines like Billy's " 'I get tired this. What we come?

Hunt or what?'" (374) are indubitably funny. Less has been said, however, about the ways in which the humor in this passage functions like comic relief in a well-crafted Elizabethan tragedy, raising serious issues of racism and acculturation integral to the tragic significance of "Fathers and Sons." Both Nick's posturing like Kit Carson in a dime Western, and Billy and Trudy's preposterous and easily exploited sexual naiveté, provide thematic counterpoint for the elegiac meditation on "how [Indians] ended" that will conclude the story. Rough comedy allows Hemingway to explore aspects of the very real plight of the Ojibway without oversentimentalizing it.

For instance, Nick, an already fallen Adam who has in spite of himself imbibed his father's Victorianism (another aspect of the tragicomedy), is the serpent in the Ojibway Eden. Billy and Trudy are unselfconscious about sexuality; Nick is ashamed and wants Billy to go away. Billy is willing to share his sister with Nick; Nick threatens to kill Billy's half-brother Eddie Gilby if he "even speaks" to Nick's own sister, Dorothy. Trudy does not comprehend the idea of miscegenation; Nick thinks of Eddie as a "half-breed" (373). Nick "happily" imagines himself as oppressor, his foot on the chest of the slain Eddie Gilby, "pleased with the picture" of himself as an Indian killer (373).

Before the passage ends, Billy is "very depressed" by his introduction to the white male's sexual double standard for men of other races. Even Trudy's exaggerated response ("No kill him! No kill him! No kill him! No! No! No!" [373]) to Nick's bogus threats suggests a prior experience of racial violence underlying her comic conviction that Nick might really kill Eddie for approaching his sister. Her rubbing contentedly against Nick and asking, with an innocent interest in procreation, "'You think we make a baby?'" (374), is also disturbing, given Nick's attitude toward "half breed bastards," his careful separation of his "friends" from the home he repairs to for supper, and an assertion in the manuscript of "Fathers and Sons" that Trudy "[had] a baby went away to be a hooker" (Kennedy Library/EH 382).[9] Sexual shame, the incest taboo, possessiveness, jealousy, miscegenation, segregation, perhaps even bastardy and prostitution –

Nick introduces all these ideas to the native inhabitants of the once virgin forest.

Hence the need for comic treatment to avoid bathos. Although the Ojibway traditionally observed strict codes of sexual behavior, with intercourse forbidden before marriage and the girl's brother expected to act as guardian of her chastity (Krumins 75–6), Hemingway in "Fathers and Sons" chooses to suggest instead that the pre-contact Ojibway world was a kind of sexual Eden corrupted by white mores (as opposed to white libertinism). His vision of forest lovemaking despoiled by the intrusion of "civilized" values would seem as sentimental as the old chestnut perpetrated by 17th-century playwright John Dryden – "I am free as Nature first made man,/ Ere the base laws of servitude began,/ When wild in woods the noble savage ran" [Part I: I.i] – without the leavening of bawdy humor and comic overstatement.

Yet the humor here is as black as the pelt of the squirrel Billy shoots. "'You can have the squirrel'" (374), Nick says, magnanimously permitting Billy to keep Billy's own kill. The joke is that Nick's characteristically white "generosity" consists of awarding a dead squirrel as the Ojibways' sole compensation for Billy's dismissal and Trudy's sexual favors. If the comedy in this passage seems racist or nasty, as it may to some contemporary readers, recall Nick's earlier, perhaps confessional assertion about the cruelty of sentimental people (370), who may mask the extent of their caring with crude humor, and his later reflection that "no[t] any jokes" about the Indians can take away the love he felt for them (376).

"Fathers and Sons" again attempts to shift away from guilty remembrance, with this curious sentence: "Now, as he rode along the highway in the car and it was getting dark, Nick was all through thinking about his father" (374), as if, in thinking about his betrayal and exploitation of the Ojibway, he had been thinking about his father instead. What's more, Nick is far from "all through." His father is never more present than in the passage that follows, one of the most beautiful in the Hemingway canon, when Nick projects his love for his father onto his passion for the natural world, and transmutes his grief for his father into mourning for the passing of rural America:

His father came back to him in the fall of the year, or in the early spring when there had been jacksnipe on the prairie, or when he saw shocks of corn, or when he saw a lake, or if ever he saw a horse and buggy, or when he saw, or heard, wild geese, or in a duck blind; remembering the time an eagle dropped through the whirling snow to strike a canvas-covered decoy, rising, his wings beating, the talons caught in the canvas. His father was with him, suddenly, in deserted orchards and in new-plowed fields, in thickets, on small hills, or when going through dead grass, whenever splitting wood or hauling water, by grist mills, cider mills, and dams and always with open fires. (375)

When Nick insists, at the end of this passage, that "after he was fifteen he had shared nothing" with his father, we suspect that that shared "nothing" is the nothing of the "nada" prayer in "A Clean, Well-Lighted Place." Father and son have clearly shared everything and its loss; have shared Aldo Leopold's "world of wounds."

The Ojibway, like many Native American cultures, practiced a puberty vision quest. A young man would be left alone on an island to seek the sympathetic attention of a particular manitou, or power being, who might be the spirit of a dead person. The manitou would visit in a dream, and would then become the young man's guide and protector through life (Teresa Smith 55–56). A visitation by an eagle, symbolic of the Thunderbirds, powerful Ojibway deities, was a potent event. Yet the Indians also believed that it was an ill omen for a seeker to receive a manitou whose power for either good or evil might overwhelm him. William Trudeau, an Ojibway elder, explains why: "because if they don't get rid of that early the one who had that vision or dream is gonna live with that monster . . . for the rest of his life and a lot of times they wouldn't live very long either. . . . [It] was better for them . . . if they could get help from those little insects or flies or birds or small animals, things like that" (quoted in Teresa Smith 57–8). The eagle of "Fathers and Sons," restless spirit of a suicide and symbol of the father's fatal "gift," may be just such a threatening manitou.

And so the eagle passage of this short story is as ambivalent as it is love-drenched. Nick is hunting when he receives his vision of the eagle dropping "through the whirling snow" (374). Concealed in a duck blind, he sees the great raptor plummet from the sky to strike "a canvas-covered decoy" (374). Hemingway, a keen amateur natural historian, certainly knew that although eagles feed primarily on fish, they also hunt waterfowl.[10] Deceived by the decoy, his talons caught in the canvas, rising with difficulty, the eagle is highly vulnerable – not the traditional symbol of empire, strength, and prowess.

What's more, the eagle is under Nick's gun during a period when hunting eagles (a sport Hemingway pursued in Idaho) was common enough. Although a few conservationists in the 1930s had begun to worry that habitat loss and overhunting might end in the eagle's extinction, raptor predation on poultry, lambs, and other small livestock nevertheless meant that the birds could be shot as varmints (Forbush and May 116–19).[11] There's nothing in the passage to suggest that Nick either fires at the eagle, or, surprised by the apparition, has time to make a conscious decision to withhold fire. There is, however, everything to suggest that the father's spirit animal – deceived, entangled, caught in Nick's sights, subject to execution as a predator on the young and helpless – is at least vulnerable to destruction by the son.

Although critics such as Richard McCann are surely right to insist that the lyrical "his father came back to him" passage "yield[s] forth the father out of the past Nick yearns for" (266), they have overlooked – perhaps because of an anachronistic sense of the eagle as an endangered species that cannot be hunted – Nick's well-camouflaged hostility fingering the trigger in the duck blind. It's at this juncture that Nick arrives at his most disturbing memory. The issues hinted at in the manuscript's suppressed rowboat passage and kindling beneath this story's surface, now burst into flame above ground in the published version. In the passage that follows Nick's vision of the eagle, we learn of a specific cruelty visited by the abused father on his son:

Nick loved his father but hated the smell of him and once when he had to wear a suit of his father's underwear that had gotten too small for his

91

father it made him feel sick and he took it off and put it under two stones in the creek and said that he had lost it. He had told his father how it was when his father had made him put it on but his father said it was freshly washed. When Nick asked him to smell of it his father sniffed at it indignantly and said it was clean and fresh. When Nick came home from fishing without it and said he lost it he was whipped for lying. (375).

There is something profoundly – and sexually – invasive in the father forcing the son into his underwear, his intimate garments, despite Nick's physical revulsion and nausea. And there is something more disturbing still in the father's "whipping" Nick, a brutal punishment, ostensibly for lying, but more accurately, for rejecting physical intimacy with his father. This is, quite simply, sexual and physical abuse and Nick, like many abused children, grows cruel in self-defense: "Afterwards he had sat inside the woodshed with the door open, his shotgun loaded and cocked, looking across at his father sitting on the screen porch reading the paper and thought, 'I can blow him to hell. I can kill him'" (375).

Nick does not kill his father with the shotgun, but the boy whipped "for lying" grows up to exact a writer's vengeance by *telling the truth* about his father in stories like the humiliating "The Doctor and the Doctor's Wife," published while Hemingway's father was still alive, a fact that resonates powerfully when we recall Nick's confession in "Fathers and Sons" that "they had all betrayed him in various ways before he died" (370). Ann Boutelle's assertion that "Fathers and Sons" is "a public confession of Hemingway's complicity in his father's suicide" (140–1) is not entirely farfetched. The story's exposure of the father's unsoundness on sex and of his abusive behavior, as well as Nick's identification with the "proud and smugly pleased" undertaker, is fraught with hostility, self-justification, and guilt.

Far from completing Nick's grief work, the underwear incident, the story's final memory of the father, is freighted with unresolved conflict:

Finally he felt his anger go out of him and he felt a little sick about it being the gun that his father had given him. Then he had gone to the Indian camp, walking there in the dark, to get rid of the smell. (375)

Although Nick does not succumb to his patricidal impulse, he adopts as his constant companion "the gun that his father had given him" as a means of sublimating his own humiliation and rage. We think of the father in "The Doctor and the Doctor's Wife" pumping shells in and out of his shotgun to assuage the shame of his emasculation, and of that story's luckless black squirrels, destined to stand in for the real objects of his rage (75). Nick has obviously learned the value of such compensatory behavior well, when, to protect himself from Billy's anger in "Fathers and Sons," he loans Billy the shotgun.

In confessing his own abnormally keen sense of smell, Nick also identifies himself with the dangerous "gift" of vision that, "surpass[ing] human requirements," has earlier in the story suggested the father's sensitivity bordering on mental illness (370). Nick's sense of smell is implicated not only in his physical revulsion from his father, but in an incestuous attraction to his sister, hinted at earlier in the jealousy Nick displays over Eddie Gilby's interest in Dorothy: "There was only one person in the family that [Nick] liked the smell of; one sister. All the others he avoided all contact with" (375).[12]

Implied here as well is Nick's revulsion from the most important of "all the others" – the mother on whom, in the manuscript, he blames his father's sexual frustration and consequent abusive behavior, and perhaps some of his own. When, also in the manuscript, Nick tells us that "there is only one thing to do" if a man is married to such a woman, and that is "to get rid of her" if "whipping" does no good, we have an explanation for the absence of wives and mothers in "Fathers and Sons" (Kennedy Library/EH 384). Nick has felt the misery of his parents' marriage so keenly that divorce and even domestic violence seem preferable to him – a stance that goes far toward explaining why he appears in this story as a single parent. Conspicuous by her absence in the published short story, the mother's presence is nonetheless felt.

When Nick heads "to the Indian camp, walking there in the dark, to get rid of the smell" of his family, he is clearly seeking to "get rid of" – to sublimate in sex with Trudy – a tremendous burden of anger and shame.[13] Yet no emotional life this tainted can be made "clean and fresh" so simply. Nick's memories, like the quail "whirring into a size you have never seen them in the air as they pass" (369), only seem to grow more overwhelming and difficult to subdue as they speed closer.

Now Nick forges an identity for himself by adopting his own spirit animal – the bird dog (375). Within the published version of the story, his choice represents the keen sensitivity and enthusiasm for the hunt that characterize Nick as a writer. His choice also works well within the context of the unpublished story – the bird dog seems an appropriate offspring for the coyote wedded to the white French poodle, a compromise between unfettered wildness and encroaching civilization. Like his father before him, Nick is "no wolf." And his totem resonates as well within the context of an Ojibway legend that Hemingway may – or may not – have known.

The legend explains that, at the time of creation, man lived in an Edenic state where all wild animals served him, speaking his language, offering themselves in sacrifice to his needs, and performing all his work. In this paradise, man had no need to hunt. Deer, moose, grouse, and geese willingly gave of their flesh. Loon and kingfisher caught fish for man, eagle and hawk hunted rabbit for him. But the animals soon grew tired of their slavery, and convened a great meeting to discuss gaining their freedom. All agreed that man should be killed, except the dog, who pleaded for mercy on man's behalf. While the other animals argued about who would undertake to kill man, the dog slunk away and warned the Ojibway of the animals' plot. But the wolf followed the dog, dragged him back to the animals' council, and accused him of treachery. The dog's punishment was to continue his servitude to man:

"Let him serve man. Let him hunger. Let him hunt for man. Let him guard man. . . . For your betrayal, you shall no longer be regarded as a brother among us. Instead of man, we shall attack you. Worse than this, from now on you shall eat only what man has left, sleep in the cold and rain, and receive kicks as a reward for your fidelity." (Johnston 50–2).

Therefore, when the other animals changed their languages, cast off their slavery to man, and dispersed to live "to ourselves, for ourselves," the dog was left behind (Johnston 52). Man, in his turn, was punished for his abuse of his animal brothers by having to hunt for his own meat.

The legend explains man's expulsion from Eden, his alienation from the natural world, and the domestication of the dog. It also lends complexity to Nick's choice of totem. With or without the explanatory legend, the bird dog, in hunting for man, is a traitor to his own kind and to wildness. From an Ojibway perspective, the perfidious hunting dog is an ideal totem for Nick, the writer who makes his living by exposing his own kith and kin, and their sacred places. Hemingway develops this theme at greater length in *The Garden of Eden*, where Davey and his dog Kibo lead the ivory-hunting father to slaughter the loved elephant, and in "The Last Good Country," where Nick's crime of selling wild trout for tourist dinners begins his flight – pursued by exploiters – into his own secret refuge, Michigan's last stand of old-growth trees.[14]

" 'What was it like, Papa, when you were a little boy and used to hunt with the Indians?' " (375). This question, emanating from Nick's own young son, startles the reader almost as badly as it startles Nick. The child has been asleep beside him on the car seat and his presence has gone unmentioned in the story until now: "[Nick] had felt quite alone but this boy had been with him. He wondered for how long" (375). Nick's initial response to his son's question, " 'I don't know' " (375) is supremely ironic, considering the intensity with which Nick has been thinking about just this subject. Swiftly he constructs an abridged, bowdlerized, and age-appropriate story:

"We used to go all day to hunt black squirrels . . . . My father only gave me three shells a day because he said that would teach me to hunt and it wasn't good for a boy to go banging around. I went with a boy named

Billy Gilby and his sister Trudy. We used to go out nearly every day all one summer." (375)

The child, wise in the ways of adults, recognizes noninformation. He insists that Nick be more forthcoming, and Nick continues to supply vague and evasive answers.

> "But tell me what they were like."
> "They were Ojibways, " Nick said. "And they were very nice."
> "But what were they like to be with?"
> "It's hard to say," Nick Adams said."

Here Nick emulates his own father's nonresponse to a boy's questions about the Indians: "'When I asked him what they were like, he said he had many friends among them'" (376). But the child's interrogation does plunge Nick into one final memory:

> Could you say that she did first what no one has ever done better and mention plump brown legs, flat belly, hard little breasts, well holding arms, quick searching tongue, the flat eyes, the good taste of mouth, then uncomfortably, tightly, sweetly, moistly, lovely, tightly, achingly, fully, finally, unendingly, never-endingly, never-to-endingly, suddenly ended, the great bird flown like an owl in the twilight, only it was daylight in the woods and hemlock needles stuck to your belly. (375–6)

The deliciousness of unbridled sexuality with his Ojibway lover becomes an erotic appreciation of nature itself, a kind of sensuous merging with the primeval forest, as Nick experiences orgasm as the flight of an owl in the twilight, and ends fulfilled, with hemlock needles stuck to his belly, as though the earth itself, and not earth's feminine emblem, Trudy, had received his seed.[15] This single sentence contains Nick's sole memory of joy unalloyed, but because that memory is sexual in content, he withholds it from his son.

But this joy too is swiftly compromised by Nick's recollection of "how Indians ended," something else that is "hard to say" to a child under twelve:

> So that when you go in a place where Indians have lived you smell them gone and all the empty pain killer bottles and flies that buzz do not kill the sweetgrass smell, the smoke smell, and that other like a

fresh cased marten skin. Nor any jokes about them nor old squaws take that away. Nor the sick sweet smell they get to have. Nor what they did finally. It wasn't how they ended. They all ended the same. Long time ago good. Now no good. (376)

Paul Smith has discovered that Prudence Boulton, the actual Ojibway girl who was Trudy's original, "ended" at age sixteen when, pregnant, she and her lover Richard Castle committed suicide by taking strychnine ("The Tenth Indian" 73–4). But readers of "Fathers and Sons" do not need biographical research to know how Trudy and the other Indians ended – the scents of death and despair are in the passage. To Nick, Trudy herself smells of sweet grass, and wood smoke, and "that other like a fresh cased marten skin" (376).[16] These are the scents he seeks when he journeys to the Indian camp to "get rid of" the smell of his family. Inviting, earthy aromas – but the last reveals Trudy's destiny. To the Ojibway girl belongs the sexual odor of wild fur and fresh bodily fluids – but her totem is the pine marten, a native animal that is trapped, killed, and flayed for the beauty of its pelt.

"Dear God, for Christ's sake keep me from ever telling things to a kid. . . . For Christ's sake keep me from ever telling a kid how things are" – so Nick's father prays in the manuscript of "Ten Indians," after rather sadistically telling his young son that "Prudie" has been "threshing around" with Frank Washburn behind the Indian camp (Kennedy Library/EH 729; quoted in Paul Smith, *A Reader's Guide* 198). Kinder than his own father, Nick in "Fathers and Sons" does not tell the boy "how things are" with the Indians, nor does he disillusion the child when he asks, " 'Will I ever live with them?' " " 'I don't know. . . . That's up to you' " is Nick's gently vague reply.

But the tension between the boy's deep need to connect with his past and Nick's apparent determination never to tell a child "how things are" mounts when the boy begins to ask about his grandfather.

"What was my grandfather like? I can't remember him except that he gave me an air rifle and an American flag when I came over from France that time. What was he like?" (376)

97

Again, Nick must construct an abridged, bowdlerized, and age-appropriate story, and again, the theme is hunting:

"He was a great hunter and fisherman . . . and his father was a great wing shot too . . . he shot very quickly and beautifully. I'd rather see him shoot than any man I ever knew." (376)

Hunting seems the only element of Nick's childhood that he is comfortable in sharing with his son. The virtually sexual gratification Nick finds in shooting birds is all he has to thank his own father for:

When you have shot one bird flying you have shot all birds flying. They are all different and they fly in different ways but the sensation is the same and the last one is as good as the first. He could thank his father for that. (376)

The boy understandably longs to participate in this masculine family tradition – "How old will I be when I get a shotgun and can hunt by myself?" – and Nick promises to arm his son when he turns twelve (376). Yet in this story where flocking birds are associated with painful memories and orgasmic sexuality, guns with patricide and suicide, and hunting with sublimated rage, the promised shotgun seems a dubious "gift" for a boy on the threshold of manhood, one that may make him too full a participant in his family's history. Nick as father would be wiser to follow Robert Jordan's example in *For Whom the Bell Tolls*: Jordan deliberately drops his grandfather's Civil War pistol, his father's suicide weapon, into a deep glacial tarn on Montana's Bear Tooth plateau, up "where the wind was thin and there was snow all summer on the hills," letting nature swallow grief and end the destructive family cycle (337).

Nick's child, reared in France far from the American landscapes that are so rich a part of this story, yearns for a place where he can encounter his grandfather's spirit. Apparently raised in an Old World Catholic tradition, he naturally anticipates that the place of communion with the past will be his grandfather's tomb: "Why do we never go to pray at the tomb of my grandfather? . . . In France we'd go. I think I ought to go pray at the tomb of my grandfather." (376–7).[17] Again Nick is evasive:

"We live in a different part of the country. It's a long way from here. . . . Sometime we'll go" (376). The nature of the grandfather's death is one reason for Nick's evasions. Catholicism forbids the burial of suicides in consecrated ground; there may well be no "tomb" for the boy to visit – and even if the grandfather is Protestant, a suicide's grave is no place for a Catholic grandchild's prayers.

Nick's evasiveness has other dimensions as well. Strangely like the bullfighter in "The Mother of a Queen," who allows his mother's remains to be thrown on the public bone heap, Nick seems to find solace in *not* thinking of his father as "buried in one place" (*Complete Stories* 317). "Now she is all about me in the air, like the birds and the flowers," Paco thinks. "Now she will always be with me" (317). The Ojibway experience the world in a similar way as embracing "not only the categories of human persons and deities but of other-than-human persons as well; animals, plants, stones, shells, as well as power beings or manitouk," and, in their stories of metamorphosis, these categories are fluid and interchangeable (Teresa Smith 49). Nick's father, too, is "with him" in "jacksnipe on the prairie" and in the call of "wild geese," "with him" in "deserted orchards and in new-plowed fields, in thickets, on small hills . . . and always with open fires" (375). His spirit resides in the vanished and vanishing American landscapes of Nick's boyhood, landscapes Nick's own uprooted child may never experience. But his spirit also resides, like the spirit of that other dangerous manitou, Paco's mother, in the clearcut, burned over terrain of a son's damaged psyche, a place no child should have to visit.

Nick's son persists in wanting to collect his scattered patrimony at some "convenient place" for a family tomb. When Nick, playing along, rejects France as a proposed site, the boy obligingly suggests "some convenient place in America," and selects what is perhaps his own favorite American place – "Couldn't we all be buried out at the ranch?" (377). "That's an idea," says Nick. Westering is the traditional American escape from all manner of trouble. The ranch might be a worthy substitute for the ruined landscape of Michigan. But not in "Fathers and Sons," the final story of *Winner Take Nothing*, a volume also containing "Wine of

Wyoming." Readers of "Fathers and Sons" already know the West as a place despoiled by mines and oilfields, where alcoholism is endemic, where sport consists of shooting prairie dogs from the highway, and even that "pleasure" is compromised by the closeness of the houses. It's a place where the Indian woman emblematic of the land is now a monstrously fat and barren wife who spends her days in bed and feeds her husband convenience foods (*Complete Stories* 343). Most disturbing of all, from a perspective that sees hunting as a bond among generations, it's a place where "*la chasse*" – the hunt – will be gone in the boy's lifetime (354). This West offers Nick no opportunity to restore to his son the child's already squandered inheritance of the American land.

"'Well, I don't feel good never to have even visited the tomb of my grandfather'" (337). The child's final line in the story bespeaks his alienation and malaise. Exiled from his ancestral land, excluded from his father's emotional life, separated from his mother, and unable to imagine his extended family – "we all" – together except in common burial, the boy indeed has little to feel good about. This child of divorce has become, as it must pain Nick to note, "awfully practical" in his reduced expectations (377). He is also angry. Denied the forest and the Indians he longs to see, expected to wait for the coveted shotgun, barred from finding out what his grandfather was really like, the boy does not understand why he must relinquish "even" his modest wish to visit the tomb of his grandfather.

With a child's intuition, Nick's son has singled out the emblem of all that troubles his family. His repeated questions to Nick about "the tomb of my grandfather," and his refusal to let go of his need to visit it, are symptomatic of a child about to mount a relentless campaign for a highly desired object. Nick is a sufficiently experienced parent to recognize defeat. Evade and postpone the inevitable for as long as he can, the time will come when Nick must revisit with his son the irrevocable loss of the natural world that once bound generations together in shared love, and the marital unhappiness, acute sensibility, and sexual discord that tore them apart. Nick resigns himself to the not far distant moment when his son will eat of the fruit of the tree of

knowledge and be expelled from childhood's Eden. " 'We'll have
to go,' Nick said. 'I can see we'll have to go' " (377).

Epilogue

Michigan's old-growth stands of white pine and hemlock – Longfellow's "forest primeval" – represent what ecologists contemporary with Hemingway called "climax" – "a more or less stable
biotic community . . . in equilibrium with existing environmental conditions . . . the terminal stage of an ecological succession"
(Lincoln and Boxshall 86).[18] According to climax theory, such
forests, when undisturbed by man, may date their development
from the withdrawal of the Pleistocene's last glacier, some
14,000 years ago.[19] The Michigan "climax" where Nick and
Trudy fittingly make love in "Fathers and Sons" Hemingway
describes in more detail in "The Last Good Country":

> They were walking on the brown forest floor now and it was springy
> and cool under their feet. There was no underbrush and the trunks of
> the trees rose sixty feet high before there were any branches. It was cool
> in the shade of the trees and high up in them Nick could hear the breeze
> that was rising. No sun came through as they walked and Nick knew
> there would be no sun through the high top branches until nearly noon.
> (516)

Once destroyed, such forests cannot be replaced by any corporate
policy of replanting. As Michigan environmentalist David Cassuto points out, "[T]he timber company . . . will cut the original
area again as soon as it is of age" (33). Prehistoric forest like that
clearcut for hemlock bark in "Fathers and Sons" can be the
product of roughly 14,000 years of development – the lifetimes
of 420 human generations. Ecological renewal can have no
meaning within the impossibly brief grandfather-to-grandson
span of "Fathers and Sons."

That is, assuming that such renewal is possible at all. There is
consensus among ecologists that the Michigan timbering frenzy
of the late 19th and early 20th centuries permanently damaged
the regenerative capacity of the land. Michael Williams puts it
this way: "In the quest for immediate profits, the reckless and

prodigal cutting of the better grades of white and jack pine had left a slash cover on the ground that caused devastating fires, which destroyed the humus in the already poor soil and any saplings that managed to grow. Only stunted bush grew to occupy the ground in time" (234).[20] Sommers et al. agree: "Nearly every woodlot or forest stand on the present Michigan landscape has been disturbed; in many cases this disturbance brought about several changes in the composition of the woodland . . . extensive second-growth forests have been created that have no known prehistoric analogue" (86–7).

Hemingway's own ecological comprehension of the environmental disaster that took place in the country of his own and Nick Adams's boyhood was similar. The galleys of *Death in the Afternoon*, containing material composed shortly before "Fathers and Sons," reveal that he understood the loss of primeval forest as irrevocable, and comprehended second growth – the terrain Nick drives through in this story as he revisits the past in his mind – not as renewal but as the aftermath of permanent injury to the land's generative or procreative capacity.

Now the second growth is coming back where the forests were slashed and the abandoned farms are picturesque and sad like the farms of New England. Eventually they may all have writers living on them as in the east; living on abandoned farms in an abandoned country with the heart gone out of it and wondering why they don't feel more like writing. Now they plant fish in the streams and have many game wardens to protect the game that will always come back to any abandoned country; it lives in the second growth that is almost impossible to walk through and people seeing it believe they know what the forest was like. But it was not like that, and you will never know what it was like if you did not see it. Nor will you know what the heart of a country was after it is gone. (quoted in Beegel 53)

Criticism of "Fathers and Sons" reveals remarkable consensus about how to read Nick's final, resigned "I can see we'll have to go" (377). Paul Strong, in an insightful essay, asserts that "With the promised journey as a bond of their love, one is left feeling hopeful for father and son" (58). Joseph Flora, whose book *Hemingway's Nick Adams* is a superb study of thematic interactions among Hemingway's finest short stories, expresses some misgivings, but concludes "We may doubt that Nick and his son will ever visit the tomb of the grandfather . . . . nevertheless the promise is there, and it leaves us with a more mellow note" (Flora 247). Erik Nakjavani, the most theoretical and scholarly of Hemingway's psychoanalytic critics, reads Nick's final line in a similar way: "This promise salvages the past by making intelligible its natural link in memory with the present and the future" (95).[21]

An ecological reading, however, yields threat where each of these critics sees promise – for environmental devastation and family turmoil like that recorded in "Fathers and Sons" snaps the "natural link" binding past to future. When a disturbance is sufficiently acute, ecologists tell us, the land will not recover, at least not to its original state. Although what remains may evolve into a viable ecosystem of another sort – like a suburban neighborhood supporting whitetail deer – that ecosystem will bear no resemblance to what was lost (Cassuto 33–4). Ernest Hemingway, child of an ecological education and a profoundly disturbed family, was both overwhelmingly attuned to the nuances of place and less optimistic than his critics. What remains of physical and psychological terrain at the conclusion of "Fathers and Sons" is "second growth" – an ecological succession that follows the destruction by man of an earlier community (Lincoln and Boxshall 344). Nick and his son are headed down the American highway toward a diminished future with no known prehistoric analogue.

NOTES

1. Quoted in Meek 29–30.
2. This passage and succeeding passages of material excised from *Death in the Afternoon* are taken from galley proofs in the collection of the Monroe County Public Library, Key West, Florida. They have been published previously, in Beegel.
3. The term Ojibway or Ojibwe – sometimes also Chippewa – refers to a large group of Algonquian-speaking peoples. The Ottawa, Potawatomi, Menominee, and Cree tribes are considered by most

103

to be part of the Ojibway group. Although it would be most correct to call the Ojibway by the name by which they know themselves – Anishnaabe or Anishnaabeg (plural) – to avoid confusion I follow Hemingway's practice and use "Ojibway." See Teresa Smith 3–7.

4. Enrico Caruso was one of the best-known operatic voices of all time. His arrest for mashing must have caused quite a sensation in the Hemingway household; Ernest's mother, Grace Hall Hemingway, was a singer, voice teacher, and avid follower of opera. For those not up on "mashing," the verb "to mash" means "to flirt with or approach aggressively," or "to force unwanted amorous attentions on a woman." Nowadays we call it "sexual harassment." Anna Held was a starlet, known for her performances in the lavish musical comedy productions of the Ziegfeld Follies and her appearances in enticing advertisements for various products, including the milk baths supposed to be her "beauty secret."

5. By contrast, according to the *World Almanac,* only 250 million board feet of lumber were harvested from Michigan's managed, second-growth forests in 1988.

6. To understand the sheer magnitude of clearcutting in Michigan, it's helpful to know that the land area of the coterminous United States is 1,903 million acres. It is calculated that approximately 45 per cent of that area, or between 822 and 850 million acres, was covered by well-developed forest when European settlement began (Williams 3).

7. After 1921, Hemingway did not return to Michigan during his father's lifetime (Clarence Edmonds Hemingway committed suicide in 1928). He apparently made a quick visit in 1947, but no other post-1921 trips to Michigan have been recorded. In addition to the demands of his adult life elsewhere, not to mention a bitter quarrel with his mother, Hemingway's unwillingness to see the much-loved terrain of his childhood scarred by this road may have played a part in his staying away.

8. According to Paul Smith, Prudence Boulton, the original of Trudy, "was the middle child of Dick Boulton (half white half Ottawa Indian) and an unidentified woman of the Tabeshaw family. . . . There were three (some say four) children: Edward (born 1897), Prudence (born 1902–died 1918), Richard (born 1905), and an unidentified fourth, possibly William? If the events of the story have a source in the biography, I suspect it was from about 1914; this makes the Boulton siblings 17, 12, and 9 when [Hemingway] was fifteen. . . . They lived within about a half mile of the Heming-

way cottage and [Prudence] worked as a maid for Grace [Hall Hemingway, Ernest's mother]." "Comments on F&S: continued," e-mail to the author, 6 March 1996.

9. Andrew J. Blackbird, in his 1883 *History of the Ottawa and Chippewa Indians of Michigan,* asserts that "The . . . Chippewas were quite virtuous in their primitive state, as there were no illegitimate children reported in our old traditions. But . . . . this evil came to be quite frequent, for immorality has been introduced among these people by evil white persons who bring their vices into the tribes" (quoted in May and Brinks 38).

10. See Forbush and May 116–19 for a period account of the eagle's natural history.

11. Photographs at the John F. Kennedy Library show Hemingway posing with a large golden eagle shot in Idaho. By 1951, however, he publicly disapproved of hunting eagles (see "The Shot" 149).

12. Hemingway used similar language to develop an incest theme in "The Last Good Country," where Nick and his sister Littless flee into the woods together: "His sister was tanned brown and she had brown eyes and dark brown hair with yellow streaks in it from the sun. She and Nick loved each other and they did not love the others. They always thought of everyone else in the family as the others" (504). In her memoir *Ernie,* Hemingway's sister Madelaine Hemingway Miller ("Sunny") seems anxious to make it clear that she, and not Prudence Boulton – the model for Trudy in "Fathers and Sons" – was Ernest's childhood companion in the woods: "Prudence was not good looking, but a good sport, and she tagged along with her brother sometimes, as I did with mine. Though some scholars hint there was something between them, I never saw any evidence of Ernie's liking her or even wanting her along on our exploring trips or squirrel hunting jaunts" (Miller 26).

13. This language is repeated in both the manuscript and the published version of "Fathers and Sons." Nick wants to "get rid of" his mother, women like her, and the odor of his father and "others" in his family. Writing and sexual intercourse are Nick's two vehicles for "getting rid of" such things, and are thus closely aligned. Coincidentally, William Trudeau, an Ojibway, describes how tribal elders would help a vision seeker "get rid of" a dangerous manitou by scraping the boy's tongue with a cedar knife (Teresa Smith 57).

14. In "The Last Good Country," Nick's pursuers include a trigger-happy warden named Splayzey, one of the mercenaries who

helped frame an historic "stock detective" named Tom Horn in order to further the ends of land-grabbing Wyoming cattle owners (525). Ominously, Horn was wrongfully accused and hanged for the murder of a teen-aged boy, as Mr. John points out in Hemingway's story: "It was his [Splayzey's] tracks by the spring where that Nester's boy was shot that they hung Tom for" (526). Also trailing the brother and sister is the "terrible" Evans boy, who "knows too much" about Nick and his haunts (527). David R. Johnson persuasively observes that although Hemingway did not complete "The Last Good Country," foreshadowing in the existing fragment suggests that both Littless and the last stand of virgin hemlock are destined to be despoiled (317–18).

15. This is the prototype of the famous forest love scene in *For Whom the Bell Tolls,* where the white bird flies for Robert Jordan and Maria (379). The "great bird" flies again, this time through the "closed window" of a gondola, when Colonel Cantwell and Renata make love in *Across the River and into the Trees* (154).

16. Michigan's sweet grass, *Hierochloë odorata* (from the Greek *hieros,* sacred, and *chloë,* grass), grows in damp soil at the edges of woods, shores, meadows, and boggy places. Used by the Ojibway in religious rituals and in making baskets, the plant when dried retains a "vanilla-like" fragrance for many years (Lakela 52; Voss 209). The Ojibway burn sweet grass in their dwellings as an offering to their manitouk, or guardian spirits. Unlike Europeans, who believe that incense burned in a sanctified building such as a cathedral is made sacred by the space, the Ojibway, according to Teresa Smith, believe that the dwelling is made sacred by the incense: "[T]he scent of sweet grass delineates the sacrality of the Anishnaabe life world – a sacrality not confined to a building, but immanent in the natural world" (33).

17. Hemingway's working title for "Fathers and Sons" was "The Tomb of My Grandfather," a fact that suggests the thematic importance of the child's near incantatory refrain (Kennedy Library/EH 383).

18. The idea of plant formations as classifiable entities that would reach stable climax communities in given climatic environments unless radically disturbed, was the brainchild of Midwesterner Fredric E. Clements (1874–1945), an almost exact contemporary of Hemingway's father. Today, Clements's climax theory is sometimes criticized as "a rigid orthodoxy that excluded an appreciation of such complex influences as man (especially the Indians), ani-

mals, wind, fire, insects, and disease"(Williams 30). However, Clements's interpretation of forest succession was much in vogue when the early ecological education of Ernest Hemingway was underway.

19. Note that we are talking here about the age of the forest as an ecosystem, not the age of individual trees within that ecosystem. Trees, like all living things, become senescent and die. Even under ideal conditions 3,000 to 4,000 years would be an extraordinary lifespan for a tree.

20. Both Michigan's land-use history and its fire ecology have major implications for a fresh reading of "Big Two-Hearted River." To date, only Susan Schmidt, in "Ecological Renewal Images in 'Big Two-Hearted River': Jack Pines and Fisher King,'" has approached the subject, but because she mistakes as "natural and necessary for forest succession" a fire that is manmade and destructive of the land's regenerative capacity, I would argue that her reading is unnaturally optimistic (143).

21. Although it mentions "Fathers and Sons" only in passing, a recent article by Frederic Svoboda must be included here. In "False Wilderness: Northern Michigan as Created in the Nick Adams Stories," Svoboda provides an excellent historical overview of how Hemingway's Michigan was "an environment shaped, sustained, and simultaneously degraded by technology and by genteel nineteenth- and early twentieth century American culture" (15). Yet I cannot agree with Svoboda when he argues that Hemingway "romanticizes" Michigan as wilderness or "frontier" (15). The Nick Adams stories in general, and "Fathers and Sons" in particular, strike me as overwhelmingly conscious of the types of degradation Svoboda delineates so well.

Including Hemingway as a participant in the romantic American pastoral tradition embodied by Huck Finn's "lighting out for the territory" is another curious feature of Svoboda's study. In *Green Hills of Africa,* Hemingway had this to say about the conclusion to Twain's novel: "All modern American literature comes from one book by Mark Twain called *Huckleberry Finn.* If you read it you must stop where the Nigger Jim is stolen from the boys. That is the real end. The rest is just cheating" (22). As Leo Marx has pointed out, Hemingway was among the first to articulate that "lighting out for the territory" was "cheating" (340) – and the processes he saw at work in Michigan doubtless were responsible for his exchanging the pastoral dream for the environmental nightmare. Or, as he put it in the galleys of *Death in the Afternoon*, "You will find other new country and other new country and the same things happen to it all" (quoted in Beegel 53).

WORKS CITED

Beegel, Susan F. *Hemingway's Craft of Omission: Four Manuscript Examples.* Ann Arbor: UMI Research Press, 1988.

Boutelle, Ann Edwards. "Hemingway and 'Papa': Killing of the Father in the Nick Adams Fiction." *Journal of Modern Literature* 9 (1981–82):133–46.

Cassuto, David N. *Cold Running River.* Ann Arbor: University of Michigan Press, 1993.

Clements, Fredric E. "Plant Formations and Forest Types." *Proceedings, Society of American Foresters* 4 (1909): 50–63.

Cox, Thomas R., Robert S. Maxwell, Phillip Drennon Thomas, and Joseph J. Malone. *This Well-Wooded Land: Americans and Their Forests from Colonial Times to the Present.* Lincoln: University of Nebraska Press, 1985.

Dryden, John. "Almanzor and Almahide or, The Conquest of Granada by the Spaniards: Parts I and II." 1670–71. *Dryden: Three Plays.* Ed. George Saintsbury. New York: Hill and Wang, 1957, pp. 1–174.

Fiedler, Leslie A. *Love and Death in the American Novel.* Rev. edn. 1966. New York: Stein and Day, 1975.

Flora, Joseph. *Hemingway's Nick Adams.* Baton Rouge: Louisiana State University Press, 1982.

Forbush, Edward Howe, and John Richard May. *Natural History of the Birds of Eastern and Central North America.* Boston: Houghton Mifflin, 1939.

Frazer, Sir James George. *The Golden Bough.* 1922. New York: Macmillan, 1978.

Hemingway, Ernest. *Across the River and into the Trees.* New York: Charles Scribner's Sons, 1950.

The Complete Short Stories of Ernest Hemingway: The Finca Vigía Edition. New York: Charles Scribner's Sons, 1987.

Death in the Afternoon. New York: Charles Scribner's Sons, 1932.

For Whom the Bell Tolls. New York: Charles Scribner's Sons, 1940.

The Garden of Eden. New York: Charles Scribner's Sons, 1986.

"The Shot." *True* (April 1951). Reprinted in *By-Line: Ernest Hemingway.* Ed. William White. New York: Charles Scribner's Sons, 1967, pp. 417–24.

"Three Shots." *The Nick Adams Stories.* New York: Charles Scribner's Sons, 1972, pp. 13–15.

Winner Take Nothing. New York: Charles Scribner's Sons, 1933.

Jobst, Jack. "Hemingway Bids Goodbye to Youth: Childhood's End in Seney." *Hemingway: Up in Michigan Perspectives.* Ed. Frederic J. Svoboda and Joseph J. Waldmeir. East Lansing: Michigan State University Press, 1995, pp. 15–22.

Johnson, David R. "'The Last Good Country': Again the End of Something." *New Critical Approaches to the Short Stories of Ernest Hemingway.* Ed. Jackson J. Benson. Durham: Duke University Press, 1990, pp. 314–20.

Johnston, Basil. *Ojibway Heritage.* Lincoln:University of Nebraska Press, 1976.

Kolodny, Annette. *The Lay of the Land: Metaphor as Experience and History in American Life and Letters.* Chapel Hill:University of North Carolina Press, 1975.

Krumins, Eda. "Hemingway, Nick Adams, and the Indians." M.A. Thesis. University of Alberta, 1993.

Lakela, Olga. *A Flora of Northeastern Minnesota.* Minneapolis: University of Minnesota Press, 1965.

Leopold, Aldo. "The Round River." *A Sand County Almanac, with Essays on Conservation from Round River.* 1966. New York: Ballantine, 1970, pp. 188–202.

Lincoln, R. J., and G. A. Boxshall. *The Cambridge Illustrated Dictionary of Natural History.* 1987. Cambridge: Cambridge University Press, 1990.

Longfellow, Henry Wadsworth. "Evangeline: A Tale of Acadie." *Selected Poems.* Ed. Lawrence Buell. New York: Penguin, 1988.

Lopez, Barry Holstun. *Of Wolves and Men.* New York: Charles Scribner's Sons, 1978.

Marx, Leo. *The Machine in the Garden: Technology and the Pastoral Ideal in America.* New York: Oxford University Press, 1964.

May, George S. and Herbert J. Brinks. Eds. *A Michigan Reader: 11,000 B.C. to A.D. 1865.* Grand Rapids, MI: William B. Eerdmans, 1974.

McCann, Richard. "To Embrace or Kill: Fathers and Sons." *New Critical Approaches to the Short Stories of Ernest Hemingway.* Ed. Jackson J. Benson. Durham: Duke University Press, 1990, pp. 266–74.

Meek, Forrest B. *Michigan's Timber Battleground: A History of Clare County: 1674–1900.* Clare County Bicentennial Historical Committee, 1976.

Miller, Madelaine Hemingway. *Ernie: Hemingway's Sister "Sunny" Remembers.* New York: Crown, 1975.

Nakjavani, Erik. "The Fantasies of Omnipotence and Powerlessness: Commemoration in Hemingway's 'Fathers and Sons.'" *Hemingway: Up in Michigan Perspectives*. Ed. Frederic J. Svoboda and Joseph J. Waldmeir. East Lansing: Michigan State University Press, 1995, pp. 91–101.

Reimann, Lewis C. *When Pine Was King*. Ann Arbor: Edwards Brothers, 1952.

Schmidt, Susan. "Ecological Renewal Images in 'Big Two-Hearted River': Jack Pines and Fisher King." *The Hemingway Review* 9.2 (Spring 1990):142–4.

Smith, Paul. "Comments on F&S: continued." E-mail to the author. 6 March 1996.

A Reader's Guide to the Short Stories of Ernest Hemingway. Boston: G. K. Hall, 1989.

"The Tenth Indian and the Thing Left Out." *Ernest Hemingway: The Writer in Context*. Ed. James Nagel. Madison: University of Wisconsin Press, 1984, pp. 53–74.

Smith, Teresa S. *The Island of the Anishnaabeg: Thunderers and Water Monsters in the Traditional Ojibwe Life-World*. Moscow: University of Idaho Press, 1995.

Sommers, Lawrence M., with Joe T. Darden, Jay R. Harman, Laurie K. Sommers. *Michigan: A Geography*. Boulder and London: Westview, 1984.

Strong, Paul. "Gathering the Pieces and Filling in the Gaps: Hemingway's 'Fathers and Sons.'" *Studies in Short Fiction* 26.1 (Winter 1989):49–58.

Svoboda, Frederic J. "False Wilderness: Northern Michigan as Created in the Nick Adams Stories." *Hemingway: Up in Michigan Perspectives*. Ed. Frederic J. Svoboda and Joseph J. Waldmeir. East Lansing: Michigan State University Press, 1995, pp. 15–22.

Voss, Edward G. *Michigan Flora, Part I: Gymnosperms and Monocots*. Bloomfield Hills Cranbrook Institute of Science and University of Michigan Herbarium, 1972.

Williams, Michael. *Americans and Their Forests: A Historical Geography*. Cambridge: Cambridge UP, 1989.

Writers' Program of the Work Projects Administration in the State of Michigan. *Michigan: A Guide to the Wolverine State*. 1941. New York: Oxford University Press, 1947.

Re-Placing Africa in "The Snows of Kilimanjaro": The Intersecting Economies of Capitalist-Imperialism and Hemingway Biography

DEBRA A. MODDELMOG

WHEN Hemingway's *The Fifth Column and the First Forty-nine Stories* was published in 1938, it began with four stories that had not previously appeared in any of his short story collections: "The Short Happy Life of Francis Macomber," "The Capital of the World," "The Snows of Kilimanjaro," and "Old Man at the Bridge." In beginning with these works, Hemingway not only emphasized their newness but also gave them a prominence of place that mirrored their prominence in his mind. He named "The Snows of Kilimanjaro" and "The Short Happy Life of Francis Macomber" among his favorite stories (Preface to *The First Forty-nine*). Critics have generally agreed that these two stories are among Hemingway's best, if not his very best. They have also insisted that these two stories, both published initially in 1936, pulled Hemingway out of an artistic slump, confirming the genius of his 1920s fiction – such as *In Our Time* (1925), *The Sun Also Rises* (1926), and *A Farewell to Arms* (1929) – and reaffirming his entitlement to the label "major American writer."

One of the main ways in which scholars have measured the restoration of Hemingway's creative ability is to compare him to Harry, the writer-protagonist of "Snows," who is seeking to recover his "will to work" (*Complete Stories* 45). Within this critical perspective, Hemingway becomes the standard of success that Harry (according to one group of critics) finally lives up to or (according to another, larger group) fails to achieve. To reverse this view, Harry becomes the measure of either the success or failure by which Hemingway's artistic powers are affirmed. For example, Scott Macdonald declares that "the achievement represented by the writing of 'The Snows of Kilimanjaro' is itself the ultimate standard against which the reader can measure Harry's failure" (72). Similarly, Gennaro Santangelo writes that the "ultimate irony" of "Snows" is that "the achieved story itself denies its possible premises"; for in contrast to Harry's lack of discipline and his fakery, Hemingway has dedicated himself to his craft and written "a great work" (261).

Comparing Hemingway to one of his characters, or vice versa, is not unusual within Hemingway criticism; indeed, rare is the critic who avoids such a practice. As Jackson J. Benson states, "it would seem that it has been nearly impossible to write at length about the fiction of Ernest Hemingway without referring to the author's life and ultimately mixing the fiction and the life together" (155–6). Hemingway himself encouraged such an approach to "Snows" when he supposedly told A. E. Hotchner, "Never wrote so directly about myself as in that story" (Hotchner 176). Hemingway turned his directness into indirectness when he apparently stated that the portrait of the artist in "Snows" presents him as he might have been (Baker 289). Contemporary critics have not abandoned the biographical approach to "Snows." For example, Kenneth Johnston declares that the story has "a firm autobiographical base, and it may be read as a report on the artistic and spiritual health of its author" (224). Yet such statements assert that we can know Hemingway "as he was," and this is a position I take issue with in this essay.

Perhaps unexpectedly, I do not suggest that we should curb our tendency to read Hemingway into his work. Such a tendency is nearly impossible to avoid and, even if we could, would have unfortunate side effects. Instead, I argue that the figure we know as "Ernest Hemingway" is always a construction and that our business as readers is to become more conscious of how Hemingway has been constructed and of the cultural assumptions that make certain constructions possible and prohibit others. Such a recognition subsequently enables us to see how a particular construction directs, although it need not totally control, our reading of Hemingway's fiction.

To illustrate this thesis, I look at how the construction of Hemingway as a "great American writer" who revived his reputation with the writing of "The Snows of Kilimanjaro" has subtended most readings of Harry's drama of individuation. My point is that the reasoning which underlies this particular construction of Hemingway is complicit with the reasoning that allows Harry to stage his drama on the backs of African Others without realizing that he is doing so or what that means for his moral stocktaking. Paris, Constantinople, Austria, Italy, Wyoming, and Michigan might be the locations to which Harry returns during his psychic journey, but the true setting of his story is the plains of East Africa with capitalist-imperialism so permeating the stage as to be invisible, as any ideology is for those whose behavior is structured by it.

It would be ridiculous to claim that Harry has an imperialistic relationship with Africa. As an individual, he cannot have such a relationship, for imperialism involves nations. We must also acknowledge that in the 1930s, when "Snows" takes place, there was no such relationship between Africa and the United States. The country in which "Snows" is set – Tanganyika, called Tanzania today – was, however, under the colonial rule of Great Britain, one of the closest allies of the United States.[1] When I claim, therfore, that Harry's attitude toward Africa is complicit with capitalist-imperialism, I am not suggesting that he literally wants to acquire or control African territory or that he directly supports American imperialistic policies in Africa. Rather, I am referring to a state of mind that is produced by and in turn helps to produce imperialistic attitudes toward another nation and thus subjects the people of that land to dependency and domination. It is a state of mind that is shared, as I also show, by the white characters of "The Short Happy Life of Francis Macomber."

Critical Constructions of Hemingway

Michael Reynolds, a contemporary biographer of Hemingway, has recently admitted what many theorists of history and biography have been saying for some time now: "we deal all our lives in fictions. . . . It is the only game available" (172). As Reynolds puts it, "we, the scholars of the trade, have created, in our time, Ernest Hemingway" (172). Reynolds is thus suggesting that identity and history are constructed, not merely recovered. We often speak of discovering evidence, but even if we learn something previously unknown – for example, that the FBI kept track of Hemingway, something that he claimed for years but which few people believed – that "discovery" occurs only when someone perceives it as biographically relevant and relates that perception through narrative and analysis. The identity of Hemingway – or of any biographical subject, including ourselves – is thus a process of articulating into being.

Because this articulation takes the form of narrative, the biographer always tells a story, but the story does not come out of nowhere, nor is it implicit in the "facts" of the author's life. Rather, the biographer chooses a story from among the many that his or her culture makes available and selects the facts that will make this story cohere. Thus, the biographer's biography – like the historian's history – always tells two stories. The first is in the text itself and is a story of inclusion: The text includes not only the plot that the biographer selects out of many but also those particular experiences that enable this plot to come together. The other story exists only in the negative, the absent, for it is a story of exclusion: the numerous plots that the biographer rejects and those experiences that must be censored or omitted for the sake of narrative unity and ideological consistency.[2]

This practice of inclusion and exclusion in biography is "a closely monitored cultural process . . . in which the Western world's dominant structures of political, social, economic, and cultural authority are deeply implicated" (Epstein 219). The experiences and facts that the biographer identifies as legitimate and relevant to emplotting the history of an individual or a nation are also culturally inscribed and socially approved. That some experiences are censored or viewed as irrelevant shows that they, too, are culturally monitored. The inscription of experience is thus never simply a descriptive or empirical act but is always ideological, meaning that it has some kind of investment in maintaining and reproducing social power.

114

To illustrate this concept, compare the Hemingway that Carlos Baker draws in *Ernest Hemingway: A Life Story* (1969) to the Hemingway of Kenneth Lynn, *Hemingway* (1987). Although the two Hemingways share many experiences, Baker and Lynn tell different stories. Their Hemingways have different forces driving them and thus exhibit contrasting psychologies. For instance, Baker spends one page describing the "fancy" of Hemingway's mother for dressing Hemingway and his older sister, Marcelline, alike, mentioning that at the age of nine months, Hemingway was photographed in "a pink gingham dress and a wide hat ornamented with flowers" (3). But in the next sentence, Baker assures his readers that Hemingway "began to assert his boyhood during the summer of 1900" by walking alone for the first time, "roaring in a lion's voice," "riding a cane for a hobbyhorse," and storming with rage when his wishes were denied (4–5). This is a one-year-old who we can easily imagine, will become the most famous Papa of his generation.

In contrast to Baker, Lynn devotes most of a chapter ("A Peculiar Idea") to Grace Hemingway's "elaborate pretense" that Hemingway and his sister were same-sex twins (40). The larger space that Lynn gives to this episode matches the importance he sees it – and Hemingway's mother – occupying in the formation of Hemingway's identity. According to Lynn, the consequences of this twinning experience were "paradoxical and far-reaching" (38): Hemingway struggled all his life with anxiety about his masculinity and sexuality. This Hemingway, we can surmise, will be reviled or embraced for his machismo, sexism, and homophobia. Baker and Lynn approach the same data from different political and psychological perspectives, and therefore construct dissimilar Hemingways.

Biographical inscription thus involves a complex negotiation of the conscious and the repressed, the extant and the absent, the dominant and the marginalized. I have traced this practice at some length because it has much to tell us about the cultural production of authors, including Hemingway, and subsequently about the meaning we assign to authors' works. One might argue, as many critics have, that because authors pose such representational difficulties, we should limit their presence in the interpretive process, perhaps eliminating them completely. But throwing the author completely out of the picture seems to me not only irresponsible but impossible. We cannot ignore the psychological effects that biographical data and scholarship have on our perception of an author and his or her work. Such information is available everywhere: on book-jacket blurbs, in formal biographies, in literary anthology headnotes, in critical articles, in newspaper and magazine articles, in made-for-TV movies, and in film. It would be disingenuous to claim that our knowledge of this biographical material – however essentialized, contested, or temporary it might be – plays no part in our formulation of an author.

Even if we were able, by some miraculous feat of selective forgetting, to repress our encounters with the historical author, we can still find compelling reasons to recall his or her historical dimension, enabling us to account for the shaping effects on the writer of such features as gender, race, class, and sexuality. In explaining the importance of considering such features, Cheryl Walker states, "As long as gender, class, race, sexual orientation, and other forms of difference are constituted hierarchically by power politics, they will remain important features of both writing and reading. The choice to ignore such issues, in the end, serves the status quo" (113). This emphasis on the historical-social conditions in which an author lived and by which he or she was formed also has the distinct benefit of establishing a horizon of meaning for reading an author's work. It delineates those discourses an author might have access to because of who he or she is (Dyer 188), discourses that can make their way into an author's work with or without his or her conscious knowledge.

In sum, the man we know as Hemingway is a representation, a shifting, often contradictory, multi-layered portrait assembled and reassembled by many scholars, journalists, friends, family members, and the man himself. As we discern new biographical information and/or advance different perspectives about human identity and history, this portrait will shift and the lines become even thicker. Moreover, because of the many choices we make in constructing Hemingway (what "facts" to include, which plots to employ), this portrait can tell us as much about ourselves – our assumptions, our ideologies – as it does about Hemingway.

Indeed, scholars such as Sacvan Bercovitch (*The American Jeremiad* [1978]) and Rob Wilson have argued that biographies of American men and women reproduce in their very form the ideology of America. According to Wilson, the "self" the American biographer feels compelled to construct is "typically a 'representative self' . . . incarnating American social codes and norms and thereby affirming the power of liberal ideology to sacralize its own goals" (171). The individual depicted in American biographies, even those written recently, is made to embody the mission of America (a mission originally defined by white men), thus affirming, "if at times castigating, the virtues, freedoms, and goals of [the] American way" (Wilson 171). In particular, Wilson argues, American biography is grounded on "assumptions of selfhood as a conflicted drama of individuation." Such assumptions involve the idea of America as a space where the individual and the nation are "metaphorically conjoined in the quest for economic and cultural capital" (172–3).

To support his thesis, Wilson examines the construction of selfhood in selected biographies of four American writers, Wallace Stevens, William Carlos Williams, Langston Hughes, and Emily Dickinson. He could just as easily have chosen biographies of Hemingway, even those, such as Baker's and Lynn's, that seem to construct Hemingway's identity from divergent vantage points. Obviously, I don't have space to explore all Hemingway biographies (of which there are many, and more to come), nor do I have space to trace the identity construction of Hemingway in any single biography from the beginning of his life to the end. Fortunately for my purposes, the biographical construction of Hemingway during the time that he wrote "Snows" and "Macomber" demonstrates Wilson's thesis in miniature. In nearly every description of Hemingway at this time, he is portrayed as caught between fearing that his artistic powers and individuality were being corrupted by a rich wife and her rich friends and proving that fear to be unwarranted by writing "The Snows of Kilimanjaro" and "The Short Happy Life of Francis Macomber."

Hemingway emerges as *the* representative American in that

117

his Puritan work ethic redeems him from sloth and failure to live up to his potential. This redemption tautologically proves him to be worthy of the success he achieves and reaffirms the merits of American democracy. Hemingway distinguishes himself from the lazy, undeserving rich (the flaw of a society based in aristocracy) by proving that hard work and discipline do pay off (the idea that because we live in a democracy, anyone in America can find material and personal success simply by "applying" him- or herself). Moreover, because Hemingway's particular form of personal success has to do with "art," his breakthrough implies that the American political system produces great artists.

As I stated above, the critics who depict Hemingway as (at least partly) redeemed by writing "Snows" and "Macomber" are numerous. Here I enlist only a few to speak for the majority. Consider, for instance, John Raeburn's description of this time in Hemingway's life. Hemingway, Raeburn claims,

> had reached a crossroads [in the 1930s], and "The Snows of Kilimanjaro" reviewed the course which had led him there and, more important, indicated a new direction. It signified Hemingway's determination to avoid Harry's fate, to resist the seductions of the comfort and security his sale of vitality to the unworthy had gotten him, and to devote himself to scaling the peaks of Art, where one might with luck and dedication create something so mysterious and imperishable as the frozen leopard found near the summit of Mount Kilimanjaro. (207)

Kenneth Lynn asserts that

> Many factors in Hemingway's own life lay behind [Harry's] self-condemnation – his guilty sense of spending too much time playing instead of working, his fear of drinking, his consciousness of how many of the new friendships he had formed were with millionaires, his pained awareness of the inadequacy of his recent books, his realization of the destructiveness of publicity. But perhaps the most significant of all the similarities between author and protagonist was symbolized by that phrase of Harry's about trading on his talent. (430)

Nonetheless, Lynn assures us, when Hemingway wrote "Snows" and "Macomber," two brief masterpieces, he was working as well as he ever had and was "again in touch with who he actually was" (429).

Robert Fleming paints a similar picture, maintaining that Hemingway had to be aware when he wrote "Snows" that "his own career had taken a wrong turn since those days in Paris when he was considered the most promising writer of his generation" (81). But, according to Fleming, "Snows" is a "major short story" that documents his *real* growth during the 1930s" (47; emphasis added). Finally, James Mellow expresses what is by now the common representation of Hemingway, claiming that "Snows," "unquestionably the great masterpiece among his short stories" (449), was written at a time when Hemingway's reputation was "suffering at the hands of critics who complained of the effect of the Hemingway legend on his work and style" (442).

The pattern by which critics have constructed Hemingway is the pattern of success as defined by the American political system. In effect, Hemingway struggles to save himself from the temptation of laziness, inefficiency, and unproductivity, and succeeds by writing an American literary masterpiece. As can be seen from their accounts, many critics have given weight to this construction by comparing Hemingway with his protagonist, Harry, who typically serves as the failure contrasting to Hemingway's success. But, as also noted, in centering their discussions of "Snows" around this drama of success/failure, cultural production/nonproduction, and temptation/redemption, critics have invariably overlooked the imperialist implications of Harry's story. Such implications are suppressed by the very ideology used to measure Harry and Hemingway.

Africa as Fat Farm

It might seem odd, at first, to hear that Harry, his story, and his critics have remained oblivious to the nuances of American ideology when all three seem explicitly to critique capitalism, especially as it manifests itself in a fascination with accumulating material comforts and wealth. Admittedly, Harry is acutely aware of the way in which money can corrupt a person, dulling one's ability and softening the will to work so that finally one does no work at all (44). This awareness is why he has returned to Africa, "where he had been happiest in the good time of his life," for he

119

wants to "start again." He and Helen have made their safari "with the minimum of comfort" because Harry believes that without luxuries he can "get back into training" and "work the fat off his soul" (44). His attacks on Helen, their wealthy friends, and "poor Julian" (identified in the original printing of the story as F. Scott Fitzgerald), who is obsessed with the rich, seem to distinguish Harry from those who are used to a life of riches or who stand in awe of those who have them. "Your damned money," he snarls at Helen (43), and twice he calls her a "rich bitch" (43, 45). He even associates Helen's small amount of fame, her commodification by the magazines *Spur* and *Town & Country*, with death: "as he looked and saw her well-known pleasant smile, he felt death come again" (49). The rich, Harry concludes, "were dull and they drank too much, or they played too much backgammon. They were dull and they were repetitious" (53).

In his more reflective and self-conscious moments, Harry relieves Helen of blame and places it on himself. He thus ultimately ascertains that the villain in his own morality play is himself. Isn't it strange, he asks, in what is clearly a rhetorical question, that "when he fell in love with another woman, that woman should always have more money than the last one?" (45). In such moments, Harry locates the center of his value system by gauging how far he has wandered from it: "He had destroyed his talent by not using it, by betrayals of himself and what he believed in, by drinking so much that he blunted the edge of his perceptions, by laziness, by sloth, and by snobbery, by pride and by prejudice, by hook and by crook" (45). In depicting his "fall from grace," Harry establishes the moral center of the story as a critique of wealth and a celebration of hard work.

This critique has been taken up by critics as they have attempted to determine whether Harry is a successful artist, a failure, or something in between. In making this determination, most critics have focused on three elements. The first is the status and function of the italicized passages, which represent Harry's thoughts but can also be seen as evidence, or lack thereof, of his artistic abilities. In scrutinizing these passages, critics have asked such questions as: Is writing in his head "all the stories that he meant to write" (52) the same as physically writing down these stories for others to read? Is the writing in these passages *good* writing, or is it maudlin and melodramatic? Are these *stories,* or are they simply fragments of stories? The second place where critics have looked for indications of Harry's redemption is the epigraph. Is Harry leopardlike in reaching the "summit" of his artistic promise? If so, is it important that the leopard is found close to the summit but not actually at it? Can we explain, as no one else has been able to, what the leopard was seeking at that altitude? Finally, critics have sought evidence of Harry's status as artist in his penultimate vision of the mountain. Does his approach to Mount Kilimanjaro amount to Harry's apotheosis as artist, or is it a cruel delusion?

As my description of these three elements suggests, critics have taken both sides in developing their arguments for or against Harry's artistic redemption. But my point is that by becoming entrenched in the effort to measure Harry according to the American ideology of hard work, productivity, and success, we miss the larger picture. Critiquing wealth and celebrating hard work are not the same as critiquing an economic system that produces wealth at the expense of those who labor. While critics have sought to explain what the leopard was seeking near the western summit of Ngàje Ngài, the House of God, they have ignored the plight of the Africans laboring below on the East Plains of Africa.

When we look more closely at Harry's situation, we find that those who labor are at his beck and call; they are "personal boys" and a "half-baked Kikuyu driver" (41), black Africans whose subordination to the white American travelers reminds us of the intricate connections between imperialism, capitalism, and racism.[3] The most prominent African laborers in "Snows" are the personal boys who slip in and out of the picture to ensure that even if Harry and Helen's safari contains no luxury, it also contains "no hardship" (44). When Harry does suffer the hardship of gangrene, these men continue to service his and his wife's needs so as to make their discomfort as comfortable as possible. Whether lifting his cot, accompanying Helen on a shoot, carrying her "kill," fixing dinner, lighting a fire, or changing Harry's dressing, the African "boys" are present to take care of Harry and

121

Helen. The extent of their caretaking function is characterized in one small scene when Molo, Harry's "personal boy," is sitting by the side of Harry's bed and asks, "Does Bwana want?" "Nothing," Harry replies, but the offer defines their relationship (44).[4]

The importance of the black, African servant to the white, American traveler is made clear in the final pages of the story. In the penultimate scene, the rescue plane arrives with Compton ready to pilot Harry to a hospital where his leg can be treated. We discover later that this scene represents Harry's final moments alive and takes place solely in his mind. In his imagination, Harry envisions "the boys" running out to the landing area and lighting fires "at each end of the level place" (55) so that Compton will know where to set down the plane. Thus, even Harry's death requires the aid of African servants who prepare the way. In the final scene, this death has occurred, with Helen finding Harry's lifeless body and shouting for Molo to come to her aid. Only when she realizes that Harry is beyond help does she plead for Harry to help her – or himself – which he can no longer do.

The black, African servant is always in the background, coming into sight only when Harry or Helen calls to him, their voices carrying the authority of command. Reflected in this dynamic is the economy of a colonial situation in which, to quote David Spurr, "one race holds, however provisionally and uneasily, authority over another" (14). Further defining this dynamic is the fact that the black man rarely speaks, and when he does, it is in response to Harry's needs: "Yes Bwana," Molo says twice (40), and once he tells Harry, "Memsahib's gone to shoot. . . . Does Bwana want?" (44). Significantly, in the final scene, when Harry is dead, the black servant is unavailable, an absence that confirms, once and for all, the relationship of dependency that exists between the white master and the "personal boy" who cares for him. Once the master is gone, the servant disappears as well, his existence defined by the existence of the white man.

It is not only the instant availability of the black African servant that suggests the imperialist economy of Harry and Helen's situation; such an economy also surfaces in the way in which they inhabit the country. It is ironic – and telling – that

Harry believes he has stripped himself of luxuries on this safari. He and Helen never have to cook a meal, and they apparently eat well; there is liquor available (which Helen attempts to prevent Harry from drinking); there is a bath within the camp; and they have proper clothing (Helen wears jodhpurs and mosquito boots). Helen and Harry have, as far as possible, imported their home and lifestyle to Africa. As Harry says, surveying the place he and Helen have made their home: "This was a pleasant camp under big trees against a hill, with good water, and close by, a nearly dry water hole where sand grouse flighted in the mornings" (40).

One also finds imperialist thinking in Helen's and Harry's attitudes toward Africa itself. For Helen, Africa has been, with the exception of Harry's sickness, a playground: " 'I love Africa. Really. If *you're* all right it's the most fun that I've ever had. You don't know the fun it's been to shoot with you. I've loved the country' " (46; original emphasis). For Harry, Africa is "where he had been happiest in the good time of his life," a place to start again, "to work the fat off his soul" (44), in other words, a kind of fat farm where Harry can sweat out the excess of American and European decadence and wealth. Through such metaphors, we come to understand the ideology of imperialism and capitalism that fuels Harry and Helen's trip to Africa. Africa is described only to the extent that it has "use value" for the white travelers: a good place to camp, a park with plenty of game, a space for writing and for righting one's life. The only thing that Harry and Helen lack is the antiseptics that will restore Harry's health. But they do have access to a plane that might arrive in time to take Harry to a hospital. When the going gets too rough, the white American travelers can arrange to go.

One might argue that this is the point of the story: that Harry cannot work the fat of money off his soul because he has sold his soul to that very devil. Such a point seems to be implied when Harry states that the rich "were dull and they drank too much, or they played too much backgammon. They were dull and they were repetitious" (53). In repeating the idea that the rich were dull, Harry implicates himself. He repeats himself; he is rich. He is rich; he repeats himself. That this implication comes

123

in the very act of critiquing the rich indicates the internal battle that Harry is waging: He wants to believe that he is different from the rich, but in fact he is fully ensconced within an ideology of wealth. Harry is as obsessed with the rich as is "poor Julian."

But if this is the story's point – that wealth corrupts and especially corrupts the artist – then we must recognize how that point has caused, perhaps even permitted, both Harry and his readers to miss the larger picture in which capitalist-imperialism is complicit with the ideology of self-reliant individualism. As much as Harry might compare himself to the self he once was and to find his present self lacking, at no time does this soul-searching consider that his trip to Africa might rely on an ethic that requires interrogation. Harry perceives his return to Africa as an attempt to resuscitate that former, more desirable self that he was when he was young, poor, and disciplined. But Harry never sees the Africans who surround him and wait on him as anything other than beings trained to service his needs; equally important, the story gives no indication that a younger Harry saw them any differently. Africa is simply "where he had been happiest in the good time of his life, so he had come out here to start again" (44).

This lack of sight – and insight – indicates the extent to which Harry's view of Africa is structured by the ideology of capitalist-imperialism. We find the most blatant sign of this in the terms the indigenous Africans apply to Harry and Helen: "Bwana," a Swahili term meaning "master" or "boss," and "memsahib," which means "madame boss." One might contend that these African men are servants and, as such, have no part to play except to attend those who pay their wages. Yet that, too, makes the point that under capitalism, especially in its imperialistic form, the laborer becomes visible and meaningful only to the extent that he or she can produce for the capitalist boss.

Thus, as it has so many times in American and British literature written by white men, Africa becomes the stage for the white male's drama of individuation, with African natives serving as stage hands without histories or scripts of their own. It is a dynamic mirrored in another Hemingway story in *The Fifth Col-*

umn and the First Forty-nine Stories and identified as one of Hemingway's favorites, "The Short Happy Life of Francis Macomber." Once again, a white American man plays out his drama of self-actualization on African soil, this time in Kenya. Like Harry and Helen, Francis and Margot Macomber rely on the native Africans for their survival and comfort but do not question the economic system that makes these men, in effect, indentured servants.

This servitude is highlighted most clearly in a scene where Francis' "personal boy" gives Francis a curious look for having bolted from the charging lion, a transgression that is immediately handled by Robert Wilson who warns the worker he will be whipped if he continues his rude behavior. This warning foregrounds the ideology of dominance that sustains imperialism even as it points to the instabilities of that dominance. Wilson's warning makes clear that the colonized Other must never return or initiate the gaze; he or she is supposed to be the object of the gaze, never its instigator. In addition, Wilson's warning exposes the master-slave dynamic that underlies the colonialist system and reminds us, more immediately, that under British colonial rule in Kenya, the contractual relationship between employer and employee was subject to the force of criminal law (Kaniki 397).[5] When Francis asks, "Do you still have them whipped?" Wilson admits that it's illegal to beat the African workers but contends that they don't complain because they prefer the beatings to the fines, which are legal. The colonial master can administer punishment with impunity simply because he is the colonial master.

Why, I hear some of you objecting, should we focus on the Africans in the background when the obvious subjects of both stories are the white people in the foreground? However well intentioned this objection might be, its logic replicates that which has fueled capitalist-imperialism and which has enabled many of us in the United States to believe that our country does not support imperialist policies or behavior.[6] Harry, Helen, Francis, and Margot (not to mention Robert Wilson, who is British) all have a colonial relationship with the Africans who serve them, a relationship made possible by national ideologies in which the subjugation of a foreign land and its people is seen as just and ethical. To ignore this is to reproduce in our reading the privilege that lies at the heart of the colonial relationship.

Reading the Contradictory Effects of Cultural Norms

My reading of "Snows" and "Macomber" has obviously benefited from critical work in the field of postcolonial studies. A field which has recently gained widespread attention in literary and cultural circles, it has taught us to consider the extensive presence of colonialism in British and American literature. It is important to note that anti-imperialist sentiments have circulated in both the United States and Great Britain throughout the 19th and 20th centuries, so a conceptual framework for critiquing the imperialist economy of "Snows" and "Macomber" has been available ever since they were written.[7] As I stated earlier, I believe that our ability to apply such a framework has been obstructed by the particular biographical construction of Hemingway as a writer who was struggling with his own artistic individuation when he wrote these stories. Our vision has been constrained by our own national ideology. This essay has shown that the life of Hemingway, and those of his characters, Harry and Francis, have been read through that most representative of American plotlines in which the attainment of selfhood and success is seen as "a conflicted drama of individuation" (Wilson 172).

By going outside the lines of this plot, beyond the individual to the relational and the international, we have enlarged the ethical scope of Hemingway's stories. This suggests that a similar enlargement is required of our formulations of Hemingway. Beyond the fact that Hemingway spent a great deal of time in Africa and called it the "place where it pleased [him] to live; to really live" (*Green Hills* 285), what exactly is his relationship to Africa? Does it serve him metaphorically and artistically in the way that it literally serves Francis and Harry?

At the time he was writing "Snows" and "Macomber," Hemingway referred to them as his African stories.[8] In a letter to his editor, Max Perkins, dated 9 April 1936, Hemingway states that

126

he has finished a long "very exciting story *of* Africa, tentatively titled 'A Budding Friendship'" (renamed "The Short Happy Life of Francis Macomber"), and he also has "another story *of* Africa called 'The Happy Ending'" (renamed "The Snows of Kilimanjaro") (*Selected Letters* 442; emphasis added). His phrasing here is intriguing and suggests a realignment of our critical vision away from the two protagonists, Francis and Harry, and toward Africa itself. Is it possible that Hemingway wanted us to see Africa as the primary subject of both stories? As just noted, there were those in the 1930s who articulated anti-imperialist sentiments. Should we configure Hemingway as one?

He certainly realized the way in which foreigners destroy countries that they invade. He expresses such sentiments in *Green Hills of Africa,* the fictionalized nonfiction he published a year before "Snows" and "Macomber." It recounts his own African safari taken in 1933–34. Near the end of this work he states that "A continent ages quickly once we come," explaining,

The natives live in harmony with it. But the foreigner destroys, cuts down the trees, drains the water, so that the water supply is altered and in a short time the soil, once the sod is turned under, is cropped out and, next, it starts to blow away as it has blown away in every old country and as I had seen it start to blow in Canada. The earth gets tired of being exploited. A country wears out quickly unless man puts back in it all his residue and that of all his beasts. When he quits using beasts and uses machines, the earth defeats him quickly. The machine can't reproduce, nor does it fertilize the soil, and it eats what he cannot raise. *A country was made to be as we found it.* We are the intruders and after we are dead we may have ruined it but it will still be there and we don't know what the next changes are. (284–5; emphasis added)

Although Hemingway acknowledges that natives live in these invaded countries, and live harmoniously with the land, these natives quickly disappear from his account so that the land is left as the only victim of the invasion. The conflict is between the land and "us," the foreigners who "intrude" on the land and ruin it. In portraying the confrontation in this way Hemingway reveals his own inability to see the natives of the invaded country and to question the ethics of "foreign" invasion itself. He sees

127

wrong as done to the land – and, I agree, it is a terrible wrong – not to the people. By removing the natives from the scene, Hemingway thus transforms a foreign invasion into a narrative of discovery ("A country was made to be as we found it") and narrows his view of the unethical action to environmental destruction.

Hemingway repeats this logic later in the same paragraph when he states, "*Our* people went to America because that was the place to go then. It had been a good country and we had made a bloody mess of it" (285; emphasis added). This description is a prime example of the kind of thinking in which the colonizer simply eliminates indigenous peoples (in this case, Native Americans and Mexicans) from the field of vision. America has been ruined, Hemingway states, and now he will go somewhere else – like Africa. What we see in these two passages from *Green Hills of Africa* is that even though Hemingway has a rather contemporary view about the need for humans to develop an ecologically sound relationship with the environment, his approach to Africa does not critique capitalist-imperialism but emanates from it. At the time that he wrote "Snows" and "Macomber," Hemingway apparently did not hold anti-imperialist views toward Africa, at least not as expressed in his nonfiction.

His position is not so clear-cut in "Snows" or "Macomber." Because both stories criticize their white characters for embracing an American ideology of wealth, materialism, and commodification, one can argue that this encompasses their imperialist attitudes. Both stories disparage the effects of entitlement – being served, being shielded from unpleasantness, being made comfortable, commanding others – exhibited by wealthy, white American and British citizens with authority over the colonized Africans. From this point of view, both stories can be read as anti-imperialist.

In opposition to this position, one might maintain that the critique of wealth and materialism in "Snows" and "Macomber" does not include a critique of imperialism per se. The targets of both stories seem to be the people who act imperially rather than the economic and political system which oppresses racialized others for the benefit of white-dominated nations. For example,

"Snows" suggests that the younger Harry was exemplary in his poverty and work ethic, and as I've pointed out, that younger Harry, like the older Harry, was unaware of his imperialist attitude toward Africa. From this point of view, Hemingway's African stories have to do, not with capitalist-imperialism, but with a lack of integrity regarding work (Harry) and a lack of bravery (Francis). Calling these stories his "African stories" is, within this perspective, not an attempt to redirect the reader's vision but reflects a kind of artistic imperialism. Africa serves Hemingway as an imaginative space onto which he can project white characters and conflicts without considering the ethics of their occupation of Africa or the humanity of the black people who stand before them.

How then should we construct Hemingway? As anti-imperialist or imperialist? I argue that the answer is both. We can read some of Hemingway's work as indicating an awareness of the unethicalness of capitalist imperialism and of the way in which "the subjugation of the ruled also involve[s] the subjugation of the ruler" (to borrow some words from Ashis Nandy writing about George Orwell, 39). But we can read other work – even the same work – as ignoring the ethics and effects of the colonizer-colonized relationship altogether. It might seem that this ambivalence brings us no closer to representing Hemingway's ethical stance, but it actually places him in the same position as most white middle- or upper-class Americans who enjoy the privilege of thinking about or ignoring – or remaining unconscious of – our own imperialist attitudes and their effects. It places him in the same position as many of his readers.

Over the past twenty years or so, critics have pointed out the imperialism, racism, sexism, anti-Semitism, and/or homophobia of some of our most celebrated authors. Hemingway's work has been scrutinized on all counts. Critics such as Carl Eby and Toni Morrison have provided recent excellent analyses of Hemingway's use of racial/racist codes. A few critics have argued that an author's racism (or other -ism) completely discredits his work. For instance, Chinua Achebe, writing about Joseph Conrad's *Heart of Darkness*, insists that a work which condones the dehumanization of Africans and which depersonalizes a portion of the human race cannot be called a great work of art (8–9). I would never argue that we should accept racism, wherever we find it, or that we should exclude racism (or other dehumanizing practices) from our aesthetic evaluations, but it seems to me that reading racism – or imperialism, or sexism, or homophobia, or anti-Semitism – is not always obvious and that the first step in eliminating such attitudes is learning how to read them.[9] This type of reading requires that we dismantle time-honored reading habits and introduce others in their place. For instance, in her work on the Africanist presence in Hemingway and other white American writers, Morrison concludes that she is attempting "to avert the critical gaze from the racial object to the racial subject; from the described and imagined to the describers and imaginers; from the serving to the served" (90).

To some extent, this has been my project in this essay: to redirect our gaze. I hope I have not given the impression that simply bringing subordinate(d) characters into the foreground, as if we were turning Hemingway's pages inside out, is enough. Rather, my point is similar to that made by Patrick McGee in "Decolonization and the Curriculum of English," when he maintains that our discussions of literature, especially but not exclusively literature we have called "classic," should include a "grasping and responding to the 'contradictory effects' of cultural norms" (283). In the case of "Snows," "Macomber," and the common critical construction of Hemingway, my approach has involved an interrogation of the contradictory effects of the American cultural norm regarding the attainment of selfhood. Because this norm, this ideology, insists that selfhood and success are attained in very specific ways, our immersion within this ideology can prevent us from seeing how struggles toward selfhood or attempts to be successful can have unintentional, unethical consequences.

In particular, it can keep us from recognizing the way in which our achievement of success in America, especially white America, is dependent on the oppression of others, especially colored, foreign others. Whether this realization has to do with white American men and women testing themselves on African soil in the 1930s, with the writings of white American authors, or with the way in which many contemporary U.S.-based corpo-rations exploit the labor of Third World colored workers, the point is the same. As this essay has shown, an important way to expand our vision is to bring the relational into our paradigms of individualism, hard work, and success; from there, we can we begin to see the larger ramifications of our encounters with diverse peoples and with a complex ecosystem.

NOTES

1. For differing views about British imperialism in Africa, see E. A. Brett, *Colonialism and Underdevelopment in East Africa* (1973). As Brett points out, not all Britons supported British involvement in Africa; for example, the British Labour party adopted a strong line of anti-imperialist thinking during the 1920s and 1930s.

2. The process I describe here is related to Hayden White's concept of emplotment, a practice by which the historian encodes "facts" into a specific plot structure. This arrangement of a set of facts into a recognizable form allows a history to serve as a possible "object of thought." But, White notes, the historian "does not bring with him a notion of the 'story' that lies embedded within the 'facts' given by the record" because there are "an infinite number of stories con-tained therein." What the historian brings to a consideration of the record are "general notions of the *kinds of stories* that might be found there" (60; original emphasis)

3. Imperialism, capitalism, and racism have a lengthy history of coop-eration. Generally speaking, imperialism is "the practice, the theory, and the attitudes of a dominating metropolitan center ruling a dis-tant territory" (Said 9). Given this definition, the reasons why impe-rialism links up with capitalism and racism are not hard to deter-mine. In fact, Marxist proponents such as Lenin propose that imperialism emerged "as the development and direct continuation of the fundamental attributes of capitalism in general" (236). What Lenin means by this is that the more capitalism takes hold in a nation, the more that nation needs raw materials, natural resources, and cheap labor, if it is to continue to increase production and, therefore, profits. The search for raw materials expands all over the world so that eventually the nation must annex colonies to provide both resources and labor (Lenin 232). For a brief review of other theories of imperialism as it manifested itself in Africa (for example,

psychological, diplomatic, African-centered), see Uzoigwe. Uzoigwe argues that, although a number of theorists have attacked the Marxist economic imperialism theory as it relates to Africa, "more serious investigations of African history" in the period from 1880–1935 indicate that "those who persist in trivializing the economic dimension of the partition do so at their own peril" (21).

4. Toni Morrison has recently noted the extent to which black male "nurses" people the pages of Hemingway's fiction, although she doesn't explicitly mention "Snows" (see 82–4). She divides these men into two categories, the loyal and the resistant. Given their apparent willingness to care for Harry and Helen, the African men of "Snows" seem to fit the former category, but who knows what they might be saying outside the range of hearing of "Bwana" and the "Memsahib."

5. In Kenya, the labor of African workers was closely monitored, most obviously by the requirement that every African adult male carry a work pass (kipande) "on which the employer recorded, among other things, the kind of work performed, time worked and wages earned. Failure to carry, or loss of the kipande rendered Africans liable to a fine and/or imprisonment up to three months. . . . The kipande greatly restricted the African's freedom of movement. A man could not leave his job of his own accord. (Kaniki 397)

6. To a great degree, our own special brand of imperialism has been masked by such concepts as "manifest destiny," "making the world safe for democracy," and "Communist containment." Almost all the expansion of U.S. territory in the 18th and 19th centuries involved the displacement or genocide of people of color (especially Native Americans and Mexicans), actions justified by the belief that the Anglo-Saxon races were religiously, morally, politically, and intellectually superior. Thus from the beginning of U.S. history, "the task of distributing and systematizing capitalist ownership in land" (Stephanson 14) and the racist acquisition of additional territory have been closely tied. The racist underpinnings of U.S. capitalist-imperialism have not died out in the 20th century, as can be seen in the imperialistic relationships our government has forged with such places as the Philippines, Vietnam, and Central America. Nor have the ties between imperialism and capitalism been broken in an age of "deterritorialized capitalism," that is, in an age when capitalism has moved from the realm of the national marketplace to global production concentrated in large transnational corporations. The business of empire both inside and outside U.S. borders has been

tied to capitalism, and this capitalist-imperialism has frequently been bound up in racism. For a compact explanation of U.S. policies of imperialism throughout its history, see Stephanson.

7. For a collection of some of these views, both literary and nonliterary, see the two-volume *Anti-Imperialist Reader,* edited by Foner, and by Foner and Winchester.

8. This identification has been picked up by critics as well, most notably in John Howell's collection, *Hemingway's African Stories: The Stories, Their Sources, Their Critics,* which focuses on "Snows" and "Macomber."

9. In his essay on *Heart of Darkness,* Achebe states that he originally intended to conclude with some thoughts about the advantages the West might derive from Africa "once it rid its mind of old prejudices and began to look at Africa . . . as a continent of people," but he was persuaded against this conclusion when he realized "that no easy optimism was possible." The West, he determines, is pervaded by stereotypes and distortions regarding Africa, and eliminating these "unwholesome thoughts" seems a difficult task. Indeed, Achebe claims, "it may well be that what is happening at this stage is more akin to reflex action than calculated malice. Which does not make the situation more but less hopeful" (12–13). Although Achebe's essay was written twenty years ago, the situation he describes does not seem to have improved much. But a primary point of my essay is that such improvement rests partly on white Western readers learning how to read our own racism and, as a consequence, learning different ways of being in the world. These obviously are not easy tasks, but they seem infinitely preferable to the kind of easy liberalism in which white people deny that race matters. As Toni Morrison writes, the habit of ignoring race is understood to be a graceful, even generous liberal gesture. To notice is to recognize an already discredited difference. To enforce its invisibility through silence is to allow the black body a shadowless participation in the dominant cultural body. According to this logic, every well-bred instinct argues against noticing and forecloses adult discourse.(9–10)

WORKS CITED

Achebe, Chinua. "An Image of Racism in Conrad's *Heart of Darkness." Hopes and Impediments: Selected Essays, 1965–1987.* Oxford: Heinemann, 1988, pp. 1–13.

Baker, Carlos. *Ernest Hemingway: A Life Story.* New York: Charles Scribner's Sons, 1969.

Benson, Jackson J. "Ernest Hemingway: The Life as Fiction and the Fiction as Life." *Hemingway: Essays of Reassessment.* Ed., Frank Scafella. New York: Oxford University Press, 1991. pp. 155–68.

Brett, E. A. *Colonialism and Underdevelopment in East Africa: The Politics of Economic Change, 1919–1939.* London: Heinemann, 1973.

Dyer, Richard. "Believing in Fairies: The Author and the Homosexual." *Inside/Out: Lesbian Theories, Gay Theories.* Ed., Diana Fuss. New York: Routledge, 1991, pp. 185–201.

Eby, Carl. "'Come Back to the Beach Ag'in, David Honey!': Hemingway's Fetishization of Race in *The Garden of Eden* Manuscripts." *The Hemingway Review* 14.2 (Spring 1995):98–117.

Epstein, William H. "(Post)Modern Lives: Abducting the Biographical Subject." *Contesting the Subject: Essays in the Postmodern Theory and Practice of Biography and Biographical Criticism.* Ed. Epstein. West Lafayette, IN: Purdue University Press, 1991, pp. 217–36.

Fleming, Robert. *The Face in the Mirror: Hemingway's Writers.* Tuscaloosa: University of Alabama Press, 1994.

Foner, Philip S. Ed. *The Anti-Imperialist Reader, A Documentary History of Anti-Imperialism in the United States, Vol. 2: The Literary Anti-Imperialists.* New York: Holmes and Meier, 1986.

and Richard C. Winchester. Eds. *The Anti-Imperialist Reader, A Documentary History of Anti-Imperialism in the United States, Vol. 1: From the Mexican War to the Election of 1900.* New York: Holmes and Meier, 1984.

Hemingway, Ernest. *The Complete Short Stories of Ernest Hemingway: The Finca Vigía Edition.* New York: Charles Scribner's Sons, 1987.

Ernest Hemingway: Selected Letters, 1917–1961. Ed., Carlos Baker. New York: Scribner's, 1981.

Green Hills of Africa. 1935. New York: Macmillan, 1987.

Hotchner, A. E. *Papa Hemingway: A Personal Memoir.* 1966. New York: Bantam, 1967.

Howell, John. Ed. *Hemingway's African Stories: The Stories, Their Sources, Their Critics.* New York: Charles Scribner's Sons, 1969.

Johnston, Kenneth G. "'The Snows of Kilimanjaro': An African Purge." *Studies in Short Fiction* 21.3 (1984):223–7.

Kaniki, M. H. Y. "The Colonial Economy: The Former British Zones." *General History of Africa, Vol. 7: Africa Under Colonial Domination 1880–1935.* Ed., A. Adu Boahen. London: Heinemann, 1985, pp. 382–419.

Lenin, V. I. "Imperialism, the Highest Stage of Capitalism." *Essential Works of Lenin.* Ed., Henry M. Christman. New York: Dover, 1987, pp. 177–270.

Lynn, Kenneth. *Hemingway.* New York: Simon and Schuster, 1987.

Macdonald, Scott. "Hemingway's 'The Snows of Kilimanjaro': Three Critical Problems." *Studies in Short Fiction* 11.1 (1974):67–74.

McGee, Patrick. "Decolonization and the Curriculum of English." *Race, Identity, and Representation in Education.* Ed., Cameron McCarthy and Warren Crichlow. New York: Routledge, 1993, pp. 280–8.

Mellow, James. *Hemingway: A Life Without Consequences.* Boston: Houghton Mifflin, 1992.

Morrison, Toni. *Playing in the Dark: Whiteness and the Literary Imagination.* Cambridge: Harvard University Press, 1992.

Nandy, Ashis. *The Intimate Enemy: Loss and Recovery of Self Under Colonialism.* New Delhi: Oxford University Press, 1983.

Raeburn, John. *Fame Became of Him: Hemingway as Public Writer.* Bloomington: Indiana University Press, 1984.

Reynolds, Michael. "Up Against the Crannied Wall: The Limits of Biography." *Hemingway: Essays of Reassessment.* Ed., Frank Scafella. New York: Oxford University Press, 1991, pp. 170–8.

Said, Edward. *Culture and Imperialism.* 1993. New York: Vintage, 1994.

Santangelo, Gennaro. "The Dark Snows of Kilimanjaro." *The Short Stories of Ernest Hemingway: Critical Essays.* Ed., Jackson J. Benson. Durham: Duke University Press, 1975, pp. 251–61.

Spurr, David. *The Rhetoric of Empire: Colonial Discourse in Journalism, Travel Writing, and Imperial Administration.* Durham: Duke University Press, 1993.

Stephanson, Anders. *Manifest Destiny: American Expansion and the Empire of Right.* New York: Hill and Wang, 1995.

Uzoigwe, G. N. "European Partition and Conquest of Africa: An Overview." *General History of Africa, Vol. 7: Africa Under Colonial Domination 1880–1935.* Ed., A. Adu Boahen. London: Heinemann, 1985, pp. 19–44.

Walker, Cheryl. "Persona Criticism and the Death of the Author." *Contesting the Subject: Essays in the Postmodern Theory and Practice of Biography and Biographical Criticism.* Ed., William H. Epstein. West Lafayette, IN: Purdue University Press, 1991, pp. 109–21.

White, Hayden. *Tropics of Discourse: Essays in Cultural Criticism.* Baltimore: Johns Hopkins University Press, 1978.

Wilson, Rob. "Producing American Selves: The Form of American Biography." *Contesting the Subject: Essays in the Postmodern Theory and Practice of Biography and Biographical Criticism.* Ed., William H. Epstein. West Lafayette, IN: Purdue University Press, 1991, pp. 167–92.

Notes on Contributors

Susan F. Beegel is Visiting Faculty in English at the University of Idaho and editor of *The Hemingway Review,* the journal of the Hemingway Society. She is the author of *Hemingway's Craft of Omission,* editor of *Hemingway's Neglected Short Fiction: New Perspectives,* and co-editor of *Steinbeck and the Environment: Interdisciplinary Approaches.*

Nancy R. Comley is Associate Professor of English and Director of Composition at Queens College, City University of New York. She is coauthor (with Robert Scholes) of *Hemingway's Genders: Rereading the Hemingway Text* and of a number of introductory texts, including *The Practice of Writing* and *Text Book.*

Debra A. Moddelmog is Associate Professor of English and an associated faculty member of both the Women's Studies and the Comparative Studies departments at Ohio State University. She is the author of *Readers and Mythic Signs* and of articles on Hemingway, Pynchon, Faulkner, Porter, and multiculturalism.

James Phelan is Professor and Chair of the Department of English at Ohio State University. He is the editor of *Narrative,* the journal of the Society for the Study of Narrative Literature, and the author of *Beyond the Tenure Track* and three books on narrative theory, the most recent of which is *Narrative as Rhetoric: Technique, Audiences, Ethics, Ideology.*

Robert Scholes is Andrew W. Mellon Professor of English at Brown University and the author of a number of books including *Proto-*

137

cols of Reading, Semiotics and Interpretation, Structuralism in Literature, and *Textual Power*. With Nancy R. Comley, he is the co-author of *Hemingway's Genders: Rereading the Hemingway Text.*

Paul Smith was James J. Goodwin Professor of English at Trinity College and founding president of the Hemingway Society. The author of *A Reader's Guide to the Short Fiction of Ernest Hemingway* and co-author (with Robert Foulke) of *An Anatomy of Literature*, he published articles on Melville, Shelley, critical theory, and the English curriculum as well as on Hemingway's short stories. Paul Smith died of cancer in the summer of 1996, shortly after finishing his editorial work on this volume.

Selected Bibliography

A comprehensive bibliography of scholarship on Ernest Hemingway and his work is beyond the scope of this collection. The following is a list of selected works essential to further investigation of his short fiction. In addition, researchers should consult *The Hemingway Review,* a biannual journal of Hemingway studies in publication since 1981.

Contributors to this collection have used the posthumously published *The Complete Short Stories of Ernest Hemingway: The Finca Vigía Edition* Students should also take care to familiarize themselves with the short story collections published during Hemingway's lifetime and with Philip Young's edition of *The Nick Adams Stories,* which includes previously unpublished manuscript fragments (see entries under Hemingway and Young, below).

Baker, Carlos. *Ernest Hemingway: A Life Story.* New York: Charles Scribner's Sons, 1969.

Ed. *Ernest Hemingway Selected Letters, 1917–1961.* New York: Charles Scribner's Sons, 1981.

Beegel, Susan F. Ed. *Hemingway's Neglected Short Fiction: New Perspectives.* Tuscaloosa: University of Alabama Press, 1992.

Benson, Jackson J. Ed. *New Critical Approaches to the Short Stories of Ernest Hemingway.* Durham, NC: Duke University Press, 1990.

Ed. *The Short Stories of Ernest Hemingway: Critical Essays.* Durham, NC: Duke University Press, 1975.

Comley, Nancy R., and Robert Scholes. *Hemingway's Genders: Rereading the Hemingway Text.* New Haven: Yale University Press, 1994.

DeFalco, Joseph. *The Hero in Hemingway's Short Stories.* Pittsburgh: University of Pittsburgh Press, 1963.

Donaldson, Scott. Ed. *The Cambridge Companion to Hemingway.* New York: Cambridge University Press, 1996.

Selected Bibliography

Flora, Joseph M. *Ernest Hemingway: A Study of the Short Fiction.* Boston: G. K. Hall, 1989.

Hemingway's Nick Adams. Baton Rouge: Louisiana State University Press, 1982.

Griffin, Peter. *Along with Youth: Hemingway the Early Years.* New York: Oxford University Press, 1985.

Less Than a Treason: Hemingway in Paris. New York: Oxford University Press, 1990.

Hanneman, Audre. *Ernest Hemingway: A Comprehensive Bibliography.* Princeton: Princeton University Press, 1967.

Supplement to Ernest Hemingway: A Comprehensive Bibliography. Princeton: Princeton University Press, 1975.

Hays, Peter L. *A Concordance to Hemingway's In Our Time.* Boston: G. K. Hall, 1990.

Hemingway, Ernest. *The Complete Short Stories of Ernest Hemingway: The Finca Vigía Edition.* New York: Charles Scribner's Sons, 1987.

The Fifth Column and the First Forty-Nine Stories. New York: Charles Scribner's Sons, 1938; republished as *The Short Stories of Ernest Hemingway.* New York: Charles Scribner's Sons, 1954.

in our time. Paris: Three Mountains Press, 1924.

In Our Time. New York: Boni and Liveright, 1925; rev. edn. New York: Charles Scribner's Sons, 1930.

Men Without Women. New York: Charles Scribner's Sons, 1927.

Three Stories and Ten Poems. Paris: Contact, 1923.

Winner Take Nothing. New York: Charles Scribner's Sons, 1933.

Howell, John M. Ed. *Hemingway's African Stories: The Stories, Their Sources, Their Critics.* New York: Charles Scribner's Sons, 1969.

Johnston, Kenneth G. *The Tip of the Iceberg: Hemingway and the Short Story.* Greenwood, FL: Penkevill Publishing, 1987.

Kert, Bernice. *The Hemingway Women.* New York: W. W. Norton, 1983.

Larson, Kelli A. *Ernest Hemingway: A Reference Guide, 1974–1989.* Boston: G. K. Hall, 1990.

Lynn, Kenneth S. *Hemingway.* New York: Simon and Schuster, 1987.

Mellow, James R. *Hemingway: A Life without Consequences.* Boston: Houghton Mifflin, 1992.

Meyers, Jeffrey. *Hemingway: A Biography.* New York: Harper and Row, 1985.

Nagel, James. Ed. *Ernest Hemingway: The Oak Park Legacy.* Tuscaloosa: University of Alabama Press, 1996.

Ed. *Ernest Hemingway: The Writer in Context.* Madison: University of Wisconsin Press, 1994.

Reynolds, Michael S. Ed. *Critical Essays on Hemingway's In Our Time.* Boston: G. K. Hall, 1983.

Hemingway: The American Homecoming. Oxford: Basil Blackwell, 1992.

Hemingway: The 1930s. New York and London: W. W. Norton, 1997.

Hemingway: The Paris Years. Oxford: Basil Blackwell, 1989.

The Young Hemingway. Oxford: Basil Blackwell, 1986.

Rosen, Kenneth. Ed. *Hemingway Repossessed.* Westport, CT: Praeger Press, 1994.

Rovit, Earl, and Gerry Brenner. *Ernest Hemingway.* Boston: Twayne, 1986.

Scafella, Frank. Ed. *Hemingway: Essays of Reassessment.* Oxford: Oxford University Press, 1990.

Smith, Paul. *A Reader's Guide to the Short Stories of Ernest Hemingway.* Boston: G. K. Hall, 1989.

Svoboda, Frederic J., and Joseph J. Waldmeir. Eds. *Hemingway: Up in Michigan Perspectives.* East Lansing: Michigan State University Press, 1995.

Tetlow, Wendolyn E. *Hemingway's In Our Time: Lyrical Dimensions.* Cranbury, NJ: Associated University Presses, 1992.

Wagner, Linda. Ed. *Ernest Hemingway: Five Decades of Criticism.* East Lansing: Michigan State University Press, 1974.

Ernest Hemingway: A Reference Guide. Boston: G. K. Hall, 1977.

Ed. *Ernest Hemingway: Six Decades of Criticism.* East Lansing: Michigan State University Press, 1987.

Waldhorn, Arthur. *A Reader's Guide to Ernest Hemingway.* New York: Farrar, Straus, and Giroux, 1972.

Weeks, Robert P. Ed. *Hemingway: A Collection of Critical Essays.* Englewood Cliffs, NJ: Prentice Hall, 1962.

Young, Philip. *Ernest Hemingway: A Reconsideration.* University Park: Pennsylvania State University Press, 1966.

Ed. *The Nick Adams Stories.* New York: Charles Scribner's Sons, 1975.